UNDERSTANDING JESUS

UNDERSTANDING *Jesus*

50 REASONS WHY JESUS MATTERS

Andrew Hamilton, SJ

Paulist Press
New York / Mahwah, NJ

Photo/Image Credits: Part-title and cover image detail from *Christ and the Rich Young Ruler*, painting by Heinrich Hofmann. Photo by Wikimedia Commons.

Cover and book design by Lynn Else

Library of Congress Cataloging-in-Publication Data

Hamilton, Andrew (Australian Jesuit)
    Understanding Jesus : 50 reasons why Jesus matters / Andrew Hamilton, S.J.
        pages cm
    Includes bibliographical references.
    ISBN 978-0-8091-4962-9 (pbk. : alk. paper) — ISBN 978-1-58768-571-2 (ebook)
    1. Jesus Christ—Person and offices—Miscellanea. 2. Jesus Christ—Historicity—Miscellanea.
3. Catholic Church—Doctrines—Miscellanea. I. Title.
    BT203.H355 2016
    232—dc23
                                                                                    2015015610

ISBN 978-0-8091-4962-9 (paperback)
ISBN 978-1-58768-571-2 (e-book)

Published by Paulist Press
997 Macarthur Boulevard
Mahwah, New Jersey 07430

www.paulistpress.com

Printed and bound in the
United States of America

To the Melbourne Lao Catholic Community,
the best of teachers

CONTENTS

INTRODUCTION

JOURNALISTS ARE FOND OF MAKING LISTS: the best ten films, books, and songs ever, or the ten most influential people of all time. In most lists, Jesus of Nazareth comes close to the top.

That is not surprising. His story and the faith that has him at its center have influenced so many people around the world. Christians, named as followers of Christ, are found in every country.

Belief in Christ has changed many people's lives, but it has also changed the world in which we live today. Even people who have hardly heard of Jesus use the stories and sayings of Jesus in the Gospels in their everyday speech. They speak of kindly people as Good Samaritans, of wayward footballers as prodigal sons, and of people pursued by the media as being crucified.

The law, our modern commitment to human rights, and the development of democracy are also difficult to understand without seeing the way in which faith in Jesus has changed people's way of looking at the world.

Of course, the political divisions in the world today are impossible to understand unless we know how people who believed in Christ spread their faith around the world, often coming into conflict with Jews, other groups of Christians, and later with Muslims.

So, even for people without religious faith, it is important to know something about Jesus and the faith in which he is central. For Christians, it is often helpful to think of how their faith in Jesus hangs together.

In this book, with its fifty points to help us understand Jesus, we will first ask the following: What can we know about Jesus? What evidence do we have that he existed and that his life corresponded to the stories that have been told about him?

In the second part, we will ask why Jesus, who after all was executed as a criminal, was remembered by his followers, and why they handed on stories about his life to following generations. To understand this, we need to have a feel for Christian faith.

In the final part, we will reflect on the kind of life that invites people to a faith in which Jesus is central. Indeed, the way that faith in Jesus has changed people's lives lies at the heart of Jesus' influence over the last two millennia.

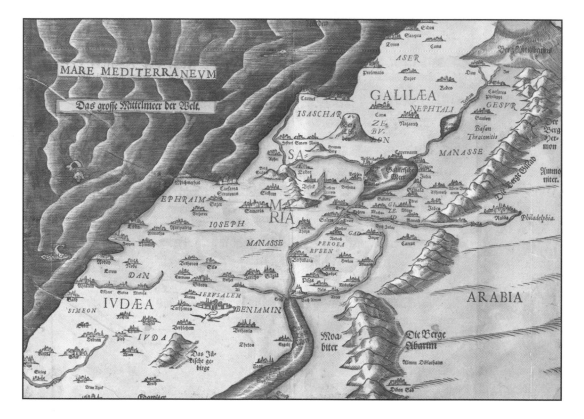

"A woodcut map of 1585 shows the Holy Land as it would have appeared at the time of Jesus, divided into Galilee, Samaria, and Judea. The map appeared in the *Itinerarium Sacrae Scripturae* (Travel book through Holy Scripture) of Heinrich Bünting (1545–1606)." From Wikimedia Commons.

PART ONE

What Can We Know about Jesus?

1. THE EVIDENCE FOR JESUS

IF WE ARE USED TO DOING Google searches or have tried to write a family history, we might be surprised to find how little evidence there is for Jesus' life apart from what his followers wrote about him.

That is not true only of Jesus. It is also the case for most people in the ancient world. They left no paper trail. There were no birth certificates, passports, shipping registers, bank accounts, or birth registers. In fact, few of the documents that officials kept have survived the centuries of war, fire, and a lack of interest in history. Even the wealthy left few traces. The son of a rural carpenter, who was executed as a criminal, left only memories.

Consequently, most of what we know about Jesus comes from people who came to believe in him, particularly from the Gospel writers, who were writing between thirty and seventy years after his death.

Apart from the Gospels, a few references to Jesus can be found in passages from Roman officials and historians. But these date from some generations after his death. He is also mentioned briefly by a Jewish historian of the uprising against Rome and its suppression, and by early Christian writers. They are generally writing to commend faith in Jesus and add little to the picture of Jesus that comes to us through the Gospels.

Archaeologists have filled out our knowledge of many people in the ancient world. Inscriptions on graves and houses, statues and urns offer names and help us to imagine how people lived. They were mostly wealthy people. For Jesus, we have only a few possible pieces of evidence, and we cannot be certain that they refer to him.

The most illuminating evidence about Jesus does not mention him at all. It describes life in Palestine at Jesus' time. By comparing what the Gospel writers and other Christian writers say about Jesus with what archaeologists have discovered about the economy and daily life at that time, and with what we know from elsewhere about the Roman government of provinces, we can test the accuracy of the Gospel stories of Jesus as well as their plausibility.

Consequently, to obtain more evidence about Jesus, we should look in more detail at the evidence for Jesus drawn from non-Christian writers, archaeology, the Gospels and other Christian writings, and from what we know about the economy and the political and religious life of Palestine at the time.

ARCHAEOLOGY AND JESUS

Modern archaeologists have shown us much about life in earlier societies. In Palestine, archaeologists have told us little about Jesus himself, but this allows us to understand the background to the stories of the Gospels.

In Galilee, for example, we now know what people bought and sold, the public buildings they erected, and what they ate and drank. We can see that it was a prosperous region and that Tiberias, in particular, was a wealthy port town. We can understand why people in Galilee resented Roman rule. There the promise of the kingdom and the payment of taxes were pressing issues that Jesus had to deal with.

2. NON-CHRISTIAN REFERENCES TO JESUS

ARCHAEOLOGICAL EVIDENCE HAS shown that the background to Jesus' life described in the Gospels is accurate. For example, a statue and inscription of Pontius Pilate has been found as well as the skeleton of a man crucified in much the same way as Jesus' crucifixion was described. Other evidence of customs in Palestine is also consistent with stories in the Gospels.

There are no relics of Jesus' time that we can refer to him with certainty. A stone box for holding the bones of the dead was discovered ten years ago, with the Aramaic inscription, "James, Son of Joseph, Brother of Jesus." But scholars believe that it was made after Jesus' time.

The fascinating Shroud of Turin, which bears the image of a crucified man believed to be Jesus, is also generally thought to come from a later date.

Non-Christian writers mention Jesus occasionally, but not from firsthand knowledge of him. They write after his death and generally rely on Christians or popular opinion for their information.

The earliest Roman reference is from Pliny, a provincial Roman official, who wrote to the Emperor in about 110 CE asking how to deal with Christians. In this letter, he refers to "Chrestus" while describing Christian practices and relies on the evidence of Christians given under interrogation.

Tacitus, a Roman historian, mentions that Nero persecuted Christians for their immorality and sedition. He claims that Christ, their founder, was executed by Pilate, so putting an end to his movement. This is valuable evidence regarding Christians, but does not provide independent knowledge of Jesus.

Suetonius, a contemporary historian of Tacitus also referred to Christians as a Jewish sect connected to Chrestus.

The references to Jesus in Jewish literature are also sparse and date from after his time. Josephus refers to Jesus as a teacher and miracle worker who drew many people to him and was accused by the rulers. He also mentions Jesus' resurrection, but this is generally thought to be added to the text by a later Christian reader.

In the centuries after Jesus' death, Jews made a collection of their oral traditions, known as the Talmud. A few passages may refer to Jesus: one to his death by hanging on the eve of Passover, after a fair trial; another refers to him as the son of Pantera, a soldier. These texts are part of the Jewish rebuttal of Christian faith.

These references are like waves lapping the edge of a large pond. They show the impact of a stone thrown into the pond, but say little of what the stone was like.

THE DEAD SEA SCROLLS

Between 1947 and 1952, a number of scrolls were discovered in caves near the Dead Sea. They date back to the time of Jesus and contain fragments of many Old Testament books and other Jewish writings. They also contain the teachings of a devout Jewish community that have some similarities to the teaching of Jesus.

For Christians interested in understanding Jesus, the Scrolls are interesting particularly because they show the variety and richness of Jewish thought in Jesus' time. In particular, they show the life of a community shaped around the hope that God was soon to free Israel.

3. CHRISTIAN SOURCES

IF WE ONLY KNEW OF JESUS from non-Christian writings, we would have heard of a Jewish man of uncertain origins, who taught, worked magic, came into conflict with other Jews, and was killed. We would also know that the source of much of this information was indirectly Christian.

Of course, we have a much fuller picture of Jesus. It is drawn from the writings of people who believed in him and became part of the Christian community. In their writings, they are not like modern historians who try to explain precisely what happened and how it came about. They want their readers to understand what faith in Jesus involves and to be more deeply committed to it.

The earliest Christian writings are the letters of St. Paul. He was a devout Jew who never knew Jesus, but initially believed that those who believed in him were traitors to the God of Israel, and therefore persecuted them. He was converted and then preached faith in Christ to Jewish and non-Jewish audiences throughout the Roman Empire. His

THE NEW TESTAMENT CANON

There were many ancient Christian writings about Jesus. The *canon*—the Greek word means a "measuring stick"—refers to those writings, believed to be inspired by God, which were the standard by which faith could be measured.

The very early Christians understood the scriptures to refer to the Old Testament books. In the first century, Paul's letters began to be collected and read. Later on, the Gospels and other works were also read in the liturgy. Churches differed in their lists but shared a common core.

When conflicting versions of the Gospel spread, partly based on different Gospels, pressure grew to draw up a list of genuine books. Church gatherings defined the list over several centuries.

letters to Christian communities focus on the significance of Jesus' death and resurrection for Christian life, but he also says that Jesus was crucified, mentions the Last Supper, and passes on some details of Jesus' teaching.

Our picture of Jesus is mainly drawn from the four Gospels that came to be recognized by the early Christians as part of Scripture. They gather stories and teachings of Jesus into a short connected story covering the last few years of his life. They describe his teaching, his miracles, and his conflicts with Jewish leaders and groups, and they give much space to his trial by the Roman authorities, his execution, and his rising from the dead.

In addition to the four Gospels, fragments of many other gospels remain, and some fairly complete texts. Many of these, mentioned by early Christian writers, have been discovered in the last two hundred years. In the versions we have, much of what they contain echoes the four Gospels, with some possible additional material. They seem mostly to be written in the second century and to reflect a version of Christian faith that was not accepted by the major churches.

References to the stories and words of Jesus are also found in other early Christian writings. They contribute to our understanding of the faith of the early Christians, but again they add little to our knowledge of Jesus.

4. FOUR GOSPELS

OUR PICTURE OF JESUS comes principally from the Gospels according to Matthew, Mark, Luke, and John. Can we rely on the picture they give of Jesus?

The difficulty in seeing the Gospels as reliable comes from what we know of the beginnings of Christianity. Jesus was a travelling teacher, who left no writings and was not accompanied by journalists. The first Gospel was not written until some thirty years after his death. The Gospel writers were not interested in sifting through the stories they had heard but in passing on accurately what faith in him meant.

So how accurately did the Gospel writers describe the life of someone who lived so long before?

The answer to this question depends on the process that led to the writing of the Gospels. It seems that faith in Christ and the stories and words about him were passed on initially by the spoken word. This is still done in many cultures today. Those who pass on stories and teachings often have memories that are prodigious by our standards. They are very creative in adapting the retelling to

THE GOSPEL GENRE

Originally, the early Christians passed on their faith by word of mouth. Preachers and teachers quoted sayings and stories about Jesus. This material was collected and treasured in the churches.

Late in the first century, this material was shaped into a continuous story of Jesus' preaching and his death. Most scholars believe that Mark's Gospel was written first, and that Luke and Matthew included sayings from another source in their Gospels. It seems that John's Gospel is largely independent of the others.

The stories in the Gospels were shaped to encourage communities struggling to live out their faith in Jesus. They became a precious resource for the churches and were read in the liturgy.

the circumstances of the hearers, but they can also be very faithful to the content of what is passed on.

When the Gospel writers were writing their works, they inherited oral traditions, and perhaps some written ones, that could have been passed down faithfully over a generation. They would then have shown the same mixture of faithfulness and creativity in adapting to the circumstances of their readers and hearers.

The Gospels are unique because they come out of a particular faith and tell a unique story, but they do have some parallels in ancient literature, particularly with biographies of the time. Ancient biographies differed from modern ones in that they showed little interest in detailed facts and the psychology of their subjects. They were very short and more interested in the big picture: conveying the importance of the subject as a model for living. Consequently, they often focused at length on the person's death. These are also features of the four Gospels.

Perhaps the best way to think of the accuracy of the Gospels is to imagine someone describing a room. They may show us accurately where the furniture is placed in the room, but will adapt their description of the furniture to the hearer's world.

5. FOUR IMAGES OF JESUS FOR FOUR COMMUNITIES

THE FOUR GOSPELS TELL basically the same story about Jesus, but they tell it in different ways. The relationship between the Gospels is complex. The Gospels according to Matthew, Mark, and Luke have much in common in the stories they tell and the words they give to Jesus, while both Matthew and Luke share additional stories and sayings that are not found in the Gospel of Mark. The Gospel of John is quite different in style and in content.

It is generally accepted that Mark's Gospel was the first to be written. Matthew and Luke relied on Mark's Gospel when writing their own Gospels, but they also introduced material from another tradition. They also adapted the material to their own purposes.

The Gospel of John is generally thought to have been written later than the others, perhaps about 80 CE. It is hard to say whether John was familiar with the other Gospels.

The Gospel of Mark is the shortest of the four. It begins with Jesus' baptism by John and God's affirmation of him as Son. It is a Gospel of conflict, full of misunderstanding and failure to follow Jesus by those with whom Jesus comes into contact. The outsiders in the Gospel—Roman soldiers and women, for example—recognize and respond faithfully to Jesus. The heart of the Gospel is that God's love is stronger than any failure on our part. It is good news in hard times.

The Gospel of Matthew is the longest of the four. Like other ancient biographies, it adds a short account of Jesus' childhood. It may have been written for Christians wrestling with their Jewish heritage. It regularly quotes Scripture to show how Jesus fulfilled the promises made to Israel, and constantly represents Jesus in debate with various groups of Jews about the right interpretation of Scripture and understanding of God. Jesus is seen as the lawgiver who insists that compassion to others is the core of serving God faithfully.

The Gospel of Luke is an expansive work, in which the story of Jesus is followed by the spread of faith in Christ, described in the Acts of the Apostles. It seems to have been written mainly for Christians from a non-Jewish background, and it is distinguished by its generous treatment of non-Christians and its emphasis on God's hospitality and our own. Jesus is described as a prophet inspired by the Holy Spirit, and it offers a model of how to live generously. Jesus' childhood is also briefly described.

The Gospel of John begins with the presence of God's Word in creation and his coming in Christ. Jesus is presented as a mysterious and God-like figure throughout the Gospel, knowing all that will happen to him and understanding God's presence in contrast to the disciples' befuddlement. The development of the story of Jesus is almost ritual—symbolic stories followed by long and meditative discursions by Jesus. Jesus' death is described as his victory, and he is always in control.

6. THE CONTEXT OF JESUS' LIFE

THE PALESTINE OF JESUS' time was part of a much larger world. It had become part of the Roman Empire, which had come to rule much of Europe, the Middle East, and modern Turkey.

Roman rule was significant for the spread of faith in Jesus because it made communications and travel relatively easy. Roman roads, the security from robbers and pirates provided by Roman troops and often brutal punishment for crime and rebellion, an advanced and uniform legal system, and the use of Greek among educated people in the Eastern part of the Empire meant that ideas and religious teaching spread easily.

These factors also placed the early Christians at risk. Complaints against Christians in one province could be forwarded to Rome and affect the lives of Christians elsewhere.

Rome was only the latest of many empires that had left their mark on Palestine. The Jews remembered their exile to Babylon. They risked being overrun by Greek religious and

JESUS' GENEALOGY

Matthew and Luke both provide us with Jesus' family tree. Matthew traces it back to Abraham, and Luke to Adam. They differ in detail, but both show Jesus to be descended from David.

Matthew includes four women. All are outsiders or are associated with disreputable conduct. Tamar bore a child to her father-in-law who mistook her for a prostitute; Rahab, a prostitute, saved the lives of Jewish spies; Ruth was a foreigner in Palestine; Bathsheba conceived a child by David, who then had her husband murdered. And Joseph wanted to divorce Mary when she became pregnant not by him.

The genealogy tells us that God works through people who were left out of family history and that God came among sinners.

philosophical ideas after Alexander the Great conquered the Eastern world. The Romans were the last occupying power.

The religious world was also diverse. The Romans were wary of the ways in which religious difference could lead to discord and rebellion. They tolerated the ancient religions of the regions they conquered provided they were morally upright and encouraged loyalty to Rome. The test of loyalty was that people throughout the empire who might worship their own Gods must also recognize the emperor as a God and worship him. Worship was a public rather than private thing.

The Romans tolerated the Jewish faith because it was ancient and the religion of a nation and ethically demanding. They overlooked the fact that Jews refused to honor images of the emperor and that they did not tolerate other forms of religious worship. Therefore, they were constantly in conflict with occupying powers that tried to introduce their own religious practices or mocked Jewish sacred practices and places.

In the thousand years surrounding Jesus' life, many of the world's great religions began. They included Buddhism, Confucianism, Taoism, and Islam. These religions did not influence Jesus directly, but they pointed to a religious ferment in the ancient world. When faith in Jesus spread into other cultures as well, it was among people familiar with responding to new religious and ethical ideas.

7. THE ROMAN OCCUPATION OF PALESTINE

IN THE CENTURY BEFORE Jesus' birth, the Jewish people had achieved a troubled independence. They endured pressure from external foes and internal conflict.

In a struggle between local rivals, both parties appealed to the Roman army for support in 63 BCE. Pompey entered Jerusalem, including the most sacred part of the temple, and Judaea became a client state of Rome. It paid taxes to Rome, and Herod was appointed as king under Roman control. Herod built massively, including the temple in Jerusalem and the port city of Caesarea. People paid heavy taxes to finance the enterprise and resented Roman rule.

After Herod's death in 4 BCE, the Romans initially appointed Herod's four sons to rule over four regions of Palestine but, shortly afterward, left Herod Antipas, son of the king, to rule the region of Galilee, while placing a Roman official (the prefect) over Judaea.

The prefect's responsibility was to raise taxes and to maintain

---

THE HERODS

In the Gospel stories, we read of two Herods: Herod Agrippa and Herod Antipas. The Romans made Herod Agrippa, whom Matthew credits with the massacre of infant boys in Bethlehem, the king of Palestine. He built the Temple of Jerusalem and appointed high priests but was never accepted by the Jewish people. They saw him as a foreigner and a Roman stooge. He died about the time Jesus was born.

Herod Antipas was one of three of Herod's sons. The Romans who appointed their own governor of Palestine gave Herod Antipas responsibility for Galilee. Gospel stories tell of him executing John the Baptist and of having a small part in Jesus' trial. He was reputedly a weak ruler and was eventually deposed.

peace in the region. He lived in Caesarea and was responsible to the Roman province of Syria where the Roman legions were quartered. He also had troops to deal with local agitation, particularly in Jerusalem where there were sporadic uprisings. Religious festivals to which visitors came to worship from outside the city were particularly tense times.

In the Gospel stories, Jesus was born while King Herod was still reigning. In the years of his preaching and death, Herod Antipas was ruler of Galilee and Pontius Pilate was prefect of the Roman province of Judaea.

The Jewish authorities had a difficult task under Roman control. People longed for the independent rule promiscd by God. They resented the tax burden imposed by the Romans and were outraged by the religious insensitivity displayed by the Roman officials. The Jewish authorities had to ensure that resentment did not lead to rebellion, and rebellion to the loss of whatever local power they had.

8. JEWISH FAITH UNDER OCCUPATION

THE CENTER OF JEWISH LIFE was the temple. In the Scriptures, it was seen as the sacred place where God dwelled with his people in the Holy of Holies. God had travelled with them on their long road to freedom and to possession of the land after their slavery in Egypt. When Jerusalem became the center of the nation, the temple was the symbol of God's presence.

The temple was the only place in which sacrifice could be offered. So people came to make sacrifices for domestic events. They also came for the major religious festivals, especially for Passover, which celebrated the delivery of the people from slavery in Egypt. Jews from outlying areas and abroad travelled for these celebrations.

Priests, who descended from a single tribe, served the temple. The temple and the Jewish local administration were supported by income from selling animals for sacrifice and by a temple tax. The administration in Jerusalem, as in other towns, consisted of the Sanhedrin, a group of elders, who in Jerusalem was led by the Chief Priest. In Jesus' time, the Roman authorities appointed the Chief Priest.

A group of wealthy Jews, the Sadducees, were also associated with the Jewish administration in Jerusalem. As in the case of the priests, the practice of their faith centered on the security and the sustainability of the temple, which in turn depended on accommodation with the Roman regime.

Throughout Judaea, people gathered for prayer and to hear the meaning of the Scriptures for their daily lives expounded by devout Jews in meeting places called synagogues. Many devout Jews would describe themselves as Pharisees. In an earlier century, the Pharisees had resisted the pressures on Jews to compromise their obedience to God's Law by adopting the customs and beliefs of the empire that had conquered them. Many died as martyrs.

In Jesus' time, the Pharisees insisted on the full observance of the Law, not simply by performing temple ritual faithfully, but also by observing the details of washing and eating in daily life. Their faith centered on exact obedience to the Law.

Outside these groups were people radically opposed to Roman rule and ready to oppose it actively. Many justified their stance on the grounds of faith, and particularly by appealing to the promises of freedom and divine rule that God had made to the Jewish people.

JEWISH FEASTS

In Jesus' time, the Sabbath was a day of rest from work and for prayer. Sacrifice in the Temple of Jerusalem was offered twice a week.

On the Feast of Passover, a lamb was sacrificed and people ate a meal to commemorate their freedom from Egypt. Jesus' death is linked to Passover.

Fifty days after the Passover, the feast of weeks marked the wheat harvest and recalled Moses' receiving God's Law. It is echoed in the Christian celebration of Pentecost (meaning "fifty").

At the Feast of Tents (or tabernacles) people came to Jerusalem waving branches. It celebrated the harvest and the Jews' nomadic life after they left Egypt.

The Day of Atonement was spent in penance and fasting. The sacrifice and sprinkling of blood in the temple became an image of Jesus' saving death.

At the Feast of Dedication, people carried branches and lit lights to recall the consecration of the altar after the temple was desecrated.

9. THE EXPECTATION OF GOD'S COMING

THE HEBREW SCRIPTURES were concerned with what God had done for Israel and what God would do in the future. They always returned to the time God had freed the people from Egypt and brought them into the promised land. This memory was also central in people's worship. God was a God who kept his promises.

Because they believed in a God who kept his promises, the faith of the people was inevitably shaken when the Assyrian Empire overran the nation and the people were expelled from their land and sent into exile in Babylon. The prophets strengthened their faith by explaining that the exile was God's response to their lack of faith, but that God was faithful to his promises. God would enable them to return to Jerusalem and would rule among them.

In the messy and unstable world that followed the people's return home, the prophets emphasized the importance of following the Law, but they spoke in increasingly dramatic ways of a time when God would come to judge the people, avenge the wrongs done to Israel and punish the compromise within it, and rule in a kingdom of peace and justice. People could look forward to the day of the Lord and prepare themselves for it by living faithfully and waiting for it.

These ideas and this thinking were current in Jesus' day and can be found in the Gospels. They led people to ask what the coming of God would look like and what signs would suggest this coming. Many people associated it with the return of the great figures of the Scriptures: Moses, who led them out of Egypt, or the prophet Elijah, who had been taken up to heaven in a chariot.

The hope that God would free the people was reflected in uprisings by people who were seen as bringing about God's reign. These were often called Zealots. The Romans brutally put down these uprisings, but the hope and the longing for the day of the Lord continued to sustain many people.

THE QUMRAN COMMUNITY

The Qumran community was derived from people who left society to live in the desert at Qumran. They separated themselves from foreigners who ruled Palestine and their own godless rulers.

A gifted leader gathered people at Qumran to form a disciplined monastic community and pray for the day when the Lord would deliver them and rule Israel. Their first monastery was burned, but around the time of Jesus' birth, they returned to the desert. They were called Essenes.

There is no evidence that Jesus was associated with this group, but some features of the early Christian churches echo its organization. They suggest the widespread hunger for the Lord's coming and the end of Roman rule.

The expectation of the Lord's coming also inspired movements that called people to reform their lives in preparation for it. In the Gospels, the most notable figure was John the Baptist, who baptized people as a sign of entry into God's kingdom and of a commitment to the just and faithful life that God asked.

For Jesus, too, the hope that God would come to rule Israel was likewise central. When speaking of God's rule, he encountered the many different expectations of what God's reign would be like.

10. JESUS AS MESSIAH

JESUS WAS A JEW; he spoke of a God who had promised to be with Israel and to free it. So when he spoke to his fellow Jews and, later, when his disciples spoke of him, they had to speak in terms that their mainly Jewish hearers would understand. They had to use the "boxes" available within their own culture. Of course, the difficulty is that no one fits comfortably into any box. The box expands or contracts to fit the person and so takes on a new meaning.

One of the boxes used to describe Jesus was the *Messiah*. In Greek, it was translated as *Christos*. When we speak of Jesus Christ, *Christ* can seem to be Jesus' given name. It is not. The *Messiah*, meaning "one who is anointed to rule," as kings and priests were anointed, was one of the figures through whom it was believed that God would come at the last days. The anointing was the work of the Spirit of God. So the title *Christ* links Jesus with that expectation.

After the exile of the Jewish people in Babylon, many prophets promised that a king or priest would come and that God would free Israel through him.

MESSIANIC CLAIMANTS

Writers of Jesus' time mention many rebellions against foreign or corrupt rulers. Some of the leaders were unstable individuals. Others, like Judas of Galilee, had political motives such as opposition to a census for taxes. These were not messianic movements—they did not see themselves acting as God's agents.

Others may have been religiously inspired. Athrongus, a slave who rebelled against Herod, saw himself as the Messiah. So may have Theudas, who led a later revolt.

These rebels attracted people to follow them, but their revolt ended in torture and death. Jesus had to dissociate himself from this kind of movement.

It was also commonly said that he would be descended from David, who was seen as the ideal King in the history of Israel.

In Jesus' time, the hope in a Messiah remained strong in many circles, along with the understanding that he would be descended from David. The hope was not universally shared, but it remained part of Jesus' inheritance.

At a time when foreign rule and influence over Judaea was so bitterly resented and thought to be offensive to God, it was inevitable that God's rescue of Israel through a Messiah would be seen in military and political terms. Once Jesus began to be seen as the Messiah, or Jesus' followers spoke of him as Messiah, people would assume that he would drive the Romans out. Because Jesus believed that God was working through him in other peaceful ways, he had to handle people's enthusiasm carefully.

Consequently, Jesus rarely describes himself as Messiah in the Gospels, and in Mark's account, he even discourages people from calling him *Messiah*. Readers need to read until the end of the Gospels to understand that Jesus was the one through whom God promised to work, and that God's way of working would lead him to being executed in Jerusalem as a criminal, not crowned as an insurgent king. He gave a new meaning to being the Messiah.

11. JESUS AS PROPHET

WHEN PEOPLE TRIED TO understand who Jesus was and what he was doing, one of the natural ways of explaining him was to say that he was a prophet. We think of prophets as wild-eyed people who told the future, usually a disastrous one. But in Jesus' world, prophets did many things.

JOHN THE BAPTIST

John the Baptist lived around the same time as Jesus. His followers are still to be found in Iraq. According to the Gospels, he lived simply in a deserted place, called on people to change their lives, and baptized them as a sign of conversion.

John baptized Jesus. That raised the question whether John was more important. The Gospels claim that John prepared the way for Jesus through whom God introduced the kingdom. John was great, but Jesus was greater.

In Mark's version, John's death echoed his way of living. Herod jailed John, who had criticized him for marrying his brother's wife, Herodias. She hated John and, when the opportunity came, she had his head cut off.

Prophets went back a long way in Israel. They spoke on behalf of God, declaring what God wanted of people in their present situation, and allowing the people to see themselves through God's eyes. They gave their messages especially to the kings and were often beaten and killed for the harsh criticism they brought.

Prophets also predicted the future. They foretold the disaster of the Babylonian defeat and exile. They also foretold the return of the exiles to Jerusalem.

They always claimed God's authority for the message they brought. They did not make themselves prophets but were called by God, often against their will. They did not simply offer their own opinions, but they had God's weight behind their words. The Spirit of God spoke through them. This authority was sometimes shown through the symbolic actions they performed, like breaking a jar to show how Israel would be broken.

Prophets appeared particularly in times of crisis, of national disaster, at times when people forgot God, and in exile. During Jesus' time, much prophetic writing foretold the day of the Lord when God would come to rule and judge the people. The prophecy was often through visions that the prophet described. Some of these visions were of violent battles between good and evil, of heavenly forces, of the trials of the just, and of God's promised victory. People were reminded that these extraordinary events were soon to come.

This kind of expectation and prophecy is called *apocalyptic*, meaning that hidden things are revealed. In Jesus' time, apocalyptic prophecy was common, as people awaited the coming of the Lord and the shaking of heaven and earth that would go with it.

John the Baptist was seen as a prophet, and Jesus had been his disciple. In the Gospels, John is described as the prophet who foretold and pointed to Jesus. Jesus also spoke authoritatively of God and acted in ways that symbolized God's rule. So it was natural to see him as a prophet.

12. JESUS AS TEACHER

IT WAS ALSO NATURAL TO describe Jesus as a teacher. He followed many other religious leaders in trying to persuade his hearers that God's coming into the world was close, and that they should change their lives to prepare for it.

Because Jesus spoke to his fellow Jews who accepted the Scriptures as God's Word, he also had to show that the way he spoke of God's actions and their response to God's invitation flowed out of the Scriptures and was consistent with what had come down from Moses and the prophets. These were the things that teachers did.

For his followers, however, Jesus was more than one among the many people who interpreted the Scriptures and their meaning for the world of their day. Jesus was unique because God was acting definitively through him. The Gospels describe this uniqueness in many ways. The crowds remark that, unlike other teachers, Jesus speaks with authority. He does not merely speak of God; God speaks and acts through him.

Jesus' teaching brought him constantly into conflict with other teachers and authorities in interpreting the Scriptures. The issues in question concerned how the details of the Mosaic Law were to be interpreted, particularly the instructions dealing with what could be done on the Sabbath as well as those about washing and eating, but the deeper issue was Jesus' authority in challenging the received teaching in the name of God's real desires and plans.

Matthew's Gospel, which may have been written for a Jewish audience, describes Jesus most often as a teacher and also brings out most strongly how he was different. He compares Jesus with the people through whom God had spoken authoritatively, including the prophets; however, he compares Jesus especially with Moses, through whom God had given the people the way of life and spelled out the relationship that was central for them. Moses was the great teacher who passed on what he had received directly from God.

THE LAW

In Jewish tradition, God gave the Law to Moses on Mount Sinai. God promised to be faithful to the people of Israel, and they promised to obey him.

The Mosaic Law became central in Jewish life after the Jews returned from exile and had to build from scratch. Ezra presented the Scriptures containing the Law to the people and they promised to be faithful to it.

Later on, scholars began to study the Law and to explain its meaning to the people. Eventually, their teaching became a resource for understanding the Law.

By Jesus' time, many people studied the Law and practiced it in detail in their daily lives. They were called Pharisees, and the Gospels describe Jesus' debates with them.

The teaching of these scholars of the Law is collected in the Talmud.

In Matthew's Gospel, Jesus is the new Moses. Like Moses, he climbs the mountain to speak authoritatively to the people about how to live and what God is like. Like Moses, he goes up a mountain and is touched by God's glory. Moses is presented as being with Jesus when God says that Jesus is the one who is to be heard. He completes and fulfills the teaching of Moses.

As with the *prophet* and *Messiah* boxes, the *teacher* box is too narrow to fit Jesus. The boxes help to understand him, but they have to be blown open to fit the presence of God within him.

13. JESUS IN CONFLICT

JESUS' LIFE ENDED IN HIS execution. As the Gospels tell the story, both the Jewish leaders and the Romans had a hand in his condemnation. Why did he arouse such opposition?

The heart of the opposition to him came from his claim that God was about to enter the world and that this was taking place through Jesus' words and actions, especially his healings and other miracles. God's day had come.

This claim disturbed the Jewish leaders, the high priests and Sadducees, because it had the potential to stir the hopes of the Jewish people for freedom from Roman rule, and thus to provoke riots and rebellion. The Romans put down such rebellions savagely.

For the high priests, too, the center of the Jewish people and their relationship with God was the temple and the worship there. Their world was not dominated by hope in the coming of the Lord. So Jesus, who was critical of the way

THE HIGH PRIESTS

In ancient Israel, priests offered sacrifice and taught. Their role was hereditary. This continued in the Temple of Jerusalem.

After the exile, high priests were chosen to coordinate temple worship. They also became leaders of the Jewish community. The high priest was important in representing authentic worship and faith against forces that corrupted it.

By Jesus' time, the Roman officials chose the high priest out of the leading families of Palestine. He was responsible for the temple and for maintaining peace under the Romans. The temple was central to the economy and religious life.

In John's Gospel, Jesus was brought for trial before Caiaphas, the high priest, and Annas, his father-in-law and the previous high priest.

the temple was run, was misguided and dangerous. He needed to be stopped before he threatened the Jewish way of life.

The Romans were concerned to maintain public order in the people whom they ruled. They feared rebellion, and thus were quick to identify potential leaders who promised independence from Rome. When Jesus spoke of the imminent rule of God and gathered followers, he was seen to be a danger.

The Pharisees believed that God was best served by faithfulness in obeying the detail of the laws and traditions that the people had received through Moses. To enter the banquet, to which God invited the faithful, you had to restrict your company to other devout people and shape the detail of your day and lives around God's commands. When Jesus ate with sinners and disobeyed the commands about eating and working, particularly on the holy Sabbath day, he was seen as blasphemous and unfaithful.

Jesus probably also disappointed the people who wanted to rebel against Rome. He refused to be co-opted into a campaign and much of his teaching was pacifist in its tone. It was more about suffering than about fighting.

Consequently, Jesus frightened some, aroused others, outraged others, and disappointed still others. In turbulent times, the life of someone who speaks and acts as Jesus did is always at risk.

PART TWO

Understanding Jesus

14. WHY WAS JESUS REMEMBERED?

IN FAMILIES, PEOPLE ARE remembered because they matter to someone. If people matter to us, we tell stories about them when we gather as families, and we make sure to pass on the most important stories to our children. We do not want the memory of our relatives to die.

If we know about people who lived in the distant past, too, it is because they mattered enough for someone to tell stories about them and for someone else to pass on those stories, and finally for someone to write the stories down. We know about people who have lived more recently for different reasons. Sometimes their names appear in official documents, sometimes their names are found in court records or in baptismal registers, and sometimes the people mean enough for others to keep passing the stories on.

Stories that are remembered do not always need to be accurate; we remember them because they sum up the person's character or significance to us. A boy who later was made king might be remembered for wearing a crown on his head

FORGETTING JESUS (LUKE 24:13–35)

Luke's Gospel tells of two people trying to forget Jesus. After he was killed, two of his followers lost hope and left town to forget about him. A stranger joined them and asked why they were sad. They told him how Jesus had died. But he explained God's plan behind Jesus' death. They invited him to join them at an inn, and he broke bread with them. They then saw that it was Jesus, and how their hearts had come alive when he spoke. They then returned to the other disciples.

They wanted to forget Jesus because they thought he was a failure. They remembered him because he became the center of their lives. He mattered.

when he came to dinner. We might wonder if he really did it regularly, but we would tell the story to others because it explains why he mattered.

All of this is true of Jesus, too. His name is mentioned because he mattered to people. They remembered things he said and passed on stories about things that he did because he was important to them. Indeed, people came together to remember him and to pray in his memory.

In time, they wrote down and gathered what they remembered of him. This helped them to pass on their memories to the next generation, and also to ensure that the different Christian groups had the same story of why Jesus mattered.

Furthermore, as the group of people whom he inspired grew in size and became noticed by other groups in society, including the civil authorities, his name appeared in legal documents and histories as the founder of the group. He became a figure in the official, written history of the world.

The central questions about Jesus, however, remain: Why did he matter to the people who first believed in him? How did he shape their lives?

15. WHY DID JESUS MATTER TO THE FIRST BELIEVERS?

IN EACH OF THE GOSPELS, there are moments of confession. These are points at which people tell Jesus why he matters to them. Peter tells Jesus, "You have the words of eternal life" (John 6:68). The centurion says of Jesus on the cross, "Truly this man was God's Son!" (Mark 15:39). These confessions always declare that Jesus is everything to people.

The Gospels were written after Jesus rose from the dead. By then, his early followers understood more clearly why he mattered. They were Jews who believed passionately that God had delivered the people of Israel from slavery in Egypt and later brought them back from exile. They longed for God's final victory over the forces of sin and enslavement. Jesus preached that God's victory was coming through his preaching and called them to change their lives radically. Those who came to believe in Jesus after his death were convinced that God's victory had now been won through Jesus and that they were called to trust in him.

SAINT PAUL

We first meet Paul hounding down Christians for betraying the God of Israel. The Acts of the Apostles tells how he was dramatically converted to Christ and became a great missionary. He founded many churches among non-Jewish people and was eventually taken for trial and executed in Rome.

Paul's great gift to the Church lay in his letters to the communities that he began. He wrote passionately of Christ, teasing out the meaning of what God has done for us through his death and resurrection, and applying it to the lives of his readers. He was warm, volatile, and totally dedicated in service of Christ and his Church.

The key to their faith in Jesus was God's raising Jesus from the dead. This convinced them that Jesus was the one whom God had promised to send to save them. They realized that God's kingdom had entered the world and that Christ would be with them until the end of time.

Their faith changed their lives in many ways. Although they continued to go to the synagogue and the Temple of Jerusalem with other Jews, they also met to pray and break the bread of the Eucharist together. The focus of their thanksgiving to God was Jesus' death and rising: God had saved them through these events. When they prayed, they prayed to Jesus as well as through him to God. They could not think of God without thinking of Jesus.

Many Jews who came to believe in Jesus, like St. Paul, found great freedom in their faith. They came to recognize that God did not only love those who were faithful to him and obeyed every detail of the Law. God came to save sinners and joined us in our sinfulness. So people lived in gratitude for God's compassion, not in fear of his rejection.

The early Christians also found strength in one another's company. They believed that the Spirit of God gathered them together and made Christ present to them. They were the beginnings of God's work in the world through Jesus, and their way of life would attract people to God's kingdom by showing what it was like.

16. WHAT DO THE STORIES OF JESUS' BIRTH SAY ABOUT HIM?

MANY CHRISTIANS CAN TELL more stories about Jesus' birth and childhood than about the rest of his life. They have seen cribs in churches, heard and sung Christmas carols, and played shepherds or angels in school plays at Christmas time. However, Jesus' childhood is mentioned in only two New Testament books: the Gospels of Luke and Matthew.

The early stories in these two Gospels are prologues to the main story of Jesus' preaching, death, and rising from the dead. Their real interest is not to offer a historical description of how Jesus was born but to explain why he mattered. In these infancy narratives, Matthew and Luke introduce the great themes of their Gospels.

In this respect, they follow the examples of Roman biographies of the time, which also include an account of the person's childhood, usually describing how their future qualities are shown in extraordinary events of their childhood.

While the stories of Matthew and Luke have common features, they differ considerably in detail. Both stories begin with announcements that Jesus will be born, who he is, and why his birth is important. In both cases, the announcement comes through angels. They are God's messengers, and so have authority. In Matthew, however, the angel comes to Joseph; in Luke, who joins the story of Jesus' birth to that of John the Baptist, the angel comes to Mary.

Both Gospels describe Jesus as the person whom God has promised to send, emphasizing his closeness to God. Both claim that he is descended from David: for Matthew, the link is through Joseph; for Luke, it is through Mary.

Matthew simply tells us that Jesus was born; Luke goes into detail. After the birth in the manger, shepherds come to see him signifying that Jesus will bring good news to the poor. Matthew brings foreign wise men, a sign that Jesus is for all nations.

Both Gospel writers tell further stories of Jesus' childhood. Luke describes Jesus being taken to the temple and being recognized as Messiah and as teacher. Matthew, who always links Jesus with details from the Old Testament, describes Jesus' flight into Egypt and return, echoing the story of Moses.

Finally, both Gospels have hints of the future suffering of Jesus—Matthew through the flight from murderous Herod, and Luke through Simeon, telling Mary that a sword will pierce her heart.

Both stories of Jesus' childhood, therefore, invite us to reflect on the meaning of Jesus.

THE CRIB

At Christmas time, most churches have cribs with Jesus, Mary, and Joseph in the stable with shepherds, Magi, and various animals.

St. Francis of Assisi, who had visited Bethlehem, asked people near Assisi to represent Jesus' birth. They made a shelter with straw for the manger, found people to be Mary and Joseph, and an ox and an ass.

As the custom became popular through Europe, statues often replaced people.

The human characters are drawn from the stories of Matthew and Luke's Gospels. The ox and the ass are drawn from a passage of Isaiah: "The ox knows its owner, and the donkey its master's crib; but Israel does not know, my people do not understand" (Isa 1:3).

17. WHY DID JESUS PREACH THE KINGDOM OF GOD?

IN THE CENTRAL PART OF the Gospels, Jesus preaches to the people and teaches his disciples. The central image of his preaching is God's kingdom. He uses little stories (parables) to explore what it means and urges people to turn to God because the kingdom is close at hand.

God's kingdom was a familiar image to Jesus' followers. In the Old Testament, it often described what the world would look like if God reigned over it. Its peace and justice contrasted with the mess that the people and their kings had made of the world. In an exiled and oppressed people, it also kept alive the hope that God would free them and would introduce a kingdom of justice and peace.

In Jesus' time, mention of the kingdom of God would have made people sit up and listen. Judaea had been incorporated into the Roman Empire, and the local authorities depended on Roman officials. Many people longed for freedom and for God to rule. God's kingdom could imply a change of regime.

JESUS' PARABLES

Like other Jewish teachers, Jesus used images and stories drawn from everyday life and stories. They are called *parables*.

Many of them are taken from everyday life—farming practices, the weather, business life. There are also best known or longer stories, like the Prodigal Son.

Parables make Jesus' hearers stop and think, and they attract them to his message. They are also told to surprise, even shock. So when someone asks Jesus who is his neighbor, Jesus tells the story of a hated and despised Samaritan acting with extraordinary generosity.

When Jesus preached the coming of God's kingdom, he drew attention to what it would be like under God's reign and how people should live when preparing for the kingdom. His preaching made them reflect on the way in which they were living.

Jesus not only spoke about God's kingdom, he also claimed that it was coming through his preaching. It was not simply an image of a just world and of faithful living. The kingdom was for real. God's intervention in the world had been promised; it was happening through Jesus' work. It could be seen in his healing of the blind and lame. It also shaped the lives of those who believed in its coming.

Jesus' preaching provoked many questions and expectations. If the kingdom were beginning, would it end with the Jewish people having control over their own nation? Would the final victory of God over evil and death soon take place?

These questions kept being asked during Jesus' life. They disturbed both the Roman and the local Jewish authorities. It was only after Jesus' death and rising from the dead that the full meaning of the coming of God's kingdom and of faith in Jesus could be seen.

18. WHY DID JESUS GATHER DISCIPLES?

WHEN JESUS PREACHED the coming of God's kingdom, he gathered many followers. Some of them stayed with him for a while, but left him later. Among those who stuck by him were many women who cared for the needs of the disciples and of the mission. It was unheard of in his day for women to have this role.

SAINT PETER

Peter was one of the twelve disciples whom Jesus called to preach and to drive out demons. Jesus appeared to the disciples after the resurrection and sent them out to proclaim that he had risen. In the Acts of the Apostles, the Holy Spirit comes down upon them, and they decide questions facing the infant Church.

Peter had a significant role in the Twelve. He was given a special role: to strengthen his brothers. He is not chosen for his gifts or virtues—he betrays Jesus and misunderstands him continually.

The early Church honored Peter for dying a martyr's death in Rome, where Paul also died. The Bishop of Rome came to take the same role in the Church as Peter.

He invited some of his followers to be his close disciples. It was common for the prophets and significant religious leaders of the Old Testament to call individuals to pass on to the people the message they had received from God, and to continue their work after they had died.

Jesus is recorded as calling twelve disciples in particular. They symbolized the twelve tribes of Israel. He took them aside to give them special teaching and sent them out as his fellow workers to preach the kingdom and to heal. They were a disparate group: they included his relatives, farmers, fishermen, political agitators, and even the despised tax collectors.

The Gospels do not describe them as heroes of the faith. They make mistakes, understand Jesus in very crude ways, are constantly put right and told off, and often display fear and ambition. One of them, Judas Iscariot, even betrays Jesus. It is clear that any success they may have in preaching the gospel is not down to them. It is entirely God's work.

The twelve remained significant after Jesus died because they had known him in his life, were the witnesses to his resurrection, and so became the privileged teachers of faith. They were the foundation stones of a new community, just as the twelve tribes of Israel were the foundation of God's chosen people.

The key to being a disciple of Jesus was to believe that God was working in him to fulfill the promises made to Israel and that God would set the people free. Believing involved more than having an opinion. It meant being so strongly convinced that you would leave family, home, and calling in order to go with Jesus. To be a disciple was not easy because they knew that they would receive the same opposition that Jesus met.

When the Gospels describe Jesus teaching his disciples, they are also speaking to the Christian communities of their day. Christians who preached the gospel would also be isolated and endure much suffering. They, too, would have to follow Jesus to Jerusalem.

19. WHY DID JESUS WORK MIRACLES?

THE GOSPELS GIVE MUCH attention to Jesus' extraordinary healings of people who were blind, lame, sick, and possessed by demons. These healings gave him a reputation for being a miracle worker. They gave authority to his words: people remarked that unlike other teachers, he taught with power.

Performing cures and doing other extraordinary deeds were not rare occurrences in Jesus' world. Such miracles were also reported of other religious figures at Jesus' time. They made more credible people's claims to speak on behalf of God and gave urgency to their invitation to follow them. They showed that God would fulfill his promises.

By contemporary standards, the stories of Jesus' miracles were not showy. They are done quietly, and Jesus always insists that they were done by the power and hand of God. God is at the center; Jesus channels God's power. In contrast, the miracles attributed to many other religious figures often highlighted the people who performed them, and sometimes filled their purses.

In the Fourth Gospel, Jesus' miracles are called *signs*. This word suggests that they did not simply demonstrate God's power over the

THE DEMONIC

Jesus is often described as healing sickness and driving out demons. Demons were seen as an important part of the world of Jesus' time. They were ultimately responsible for many of the harmful things in human life—natural disasters, mental and physical illness, and death itself.

Jesus' mission to introduce the kingdom of God involved breaking the power of the demonic world. So he drives out demons and restores possessed people to a full life. He stills storms on the sea and goes into the desert and places inhabited by demons. In John's Gospel, Satan returns at the hour of Jesus' passion.

world, but also showed what the world would look like when God ruled and so helped us to understand what God is like.

So when Jesus cured the blind and the lame, he also demonstrated that the kingdom of God would take away our spiritual blindness and reluctance to follow Jesus. When he drove out demons, he showed that the kingdom of God would conquer the forces of evil and free people from sickness. God's kingdom was about life, healing, wholeness, and freedom.

The miracles also showed what God is like. The Gospels deal fully with many of Jesus' miracles performed on the Sabbath. In Jewish life, this was the day on which God rested, and thus one on which faithful people did not work. So when he cured people, Jesus was criticized for not respecting the Sabbath. It was implied that he had no respect for God.

Jesus resisted the charge strongly. He claimed that his healings showed that God is more concerned with the health and life of human beings than with ensuring that they did not work on the Sabbath. Thus God would want people to be cured on the Sabbath. Jesus' actions showed what God is like.

20. WHAT DO JESUS' RELATIONSHIPS SAY ABOUT HIM?

IN JESUS' WORLD, everything pointed to God and to God's kingdom. So when he spoke of the coming of God's kingdom and of what that meant for people's lives, it was inevitable that his hearers would look closely at the way in which he lived. His words, his behavior at meals, the people he spoke to or avoided, and the way he behaved on the Sabbath—the day consecrated to God—would all show what God was like.

JESUS AND WOMEN

In the Gospels, women have an important and active part. God's plan depends on Mary's yes to the angel. Women travel with Jesus in his preaching and support his enterprise. When Jesus dies and his male disciples run away, the women stay by the cross and are the first to hear of his rising from the dead.

Jesus' relationship with women is also significant. He notices them, heals them, stands by them when they are humiliated, dines with them, engages in honest and playful conversation with them, and enjoys their friendship.

The place of women in the churches has often been problematic. Jesus' example does not license discrimination or paternalism.

So his hearers, particularly Jews like the Pharisees and those concerned with the interpretation of Sacred Scripture, checked to make sure that what he did and said was consistent with what they believed the Scriptures to say.

They found fault with much he said and did. Jesus himself deliberately acted in ways that challenged his critics' narrow and exclusive views of God. He believed that they concealed the real face of the God of Israel. He gave most offence by the way in which he related to people.

This was particularly true of his behavior at meals. Jewish

meals were loaded with meaning. The Scriptures spoke of the day of God's coming as a rich banquet when the righteous and faithful would sit down happily with God in plenty.

Each daily meal was a ritual event that mirrored God's banquet for the just. People observed the washings commanded by Moses, particularly those applying to the Sabbath and the prohibition of working. Most importantly, they kept company at table only with the devout and faithful, whom God would welcome into the kingdom.

By these standards, Jesus was recklessly careless in his relationships. He welcomed the company of prostitutes and the Mafiosi of his day who extorted taxes for the Roman occupiers of Palestine. These people were, by definition, excluded from God's kingdom and should have been excluded from good Jewish society.

Jesus was also cavalier in his attitude toward the people he cured. If people asked for healing and to be free from demons, he cured them, Sabbath or not. If they were ritually impure, he allowed them to touch him and he cured them. He did not respect the boundaries set out in the Scriptures.

Behind Jesus' ways of relating lay a radical understanding of God. God invited everybody to the banquet, especially those most in need and most disreputable. Furthermore, it was precisely because the Sabbath was God's day that it was a day of healing. God was a God of life.

21. WHY WAS JESUS KILLED?

THE GOSPEL ACCOUNTS suggest that the Jewish leaders plotted to kill Jesus but needed to involve the Roman Procurator, Pontius Pilate, to have him executed. They also explain that the crisis came when Jesus was visiting Jerusalem for the Passover, a feast that commemorated the liberation of the people from Egyptian rule. It was a time of heightened national religious feeling and an anxious time for Jewish and Roman authorities.

Jesus himself provoked the crisis by preaching the coming of God's rule boldly, entering the city ceremoniously on a donkey and driving sellers out of the temple in God's name. This action would have aroused hopes that Jesus was about to introduce the kingdom. It could have been the spark that led to his arrest and death.

The Gospels name many groups that wanted Jesus out of the way. To our eyes, their reasons for wanting Jesus out of the way were both political and religious. (In Jesus' time, politics were religious and religion was political). He offended Jewish groups by preaching that God's kingdom was about to come through his ministry.

PONTIUS PILATE

Pontius Pilate was the prefect of Judaea at the time of Jesus' death. He was responsible for maintaining order, appointing the high priest, and collecting taxes.

The Gospels describe Pilate as a well-meaning but weak judge, who wanted to set Jesus free but was afraid of the rioting that might ensue. John's Gospel develops his inner turmoil.

Jewish writers describe Pilate as a brutal and insensitive official, who treated Jewish customs with contempt and violently suppressed civil unrest. He was recalled to Rome for his brutality.

The early Christians may have wanted to emphasize the Jewish leaders' part in Jesus' execution, and thus softened Pilate's image for fear of offending the Romans.

Jesus also portrayed God in ways that offended them. He offended the Pharisees by proclaiming a God who invited sinners and the disreputable to the kingdom and who was, above all, compassionate rather than judgmental.

He offended the high priests by portraying a God for whom the Temple of Jerusalem was important but not central in Jewish life. He emphasized generosity of heart and trust in God as indispensable in ritual. They also feared that his preaching of God's kingdom would lead to civil unrest and to a savage Roman response.

The Gospels claim that when the high priests charged him with blasphemy, the evidence was faked. The charge recognizes, however, that the kingdom of God that Jesus preached was a radical challenge to the Jewish religious authorities.

The Gospels put most of the blame on the Jewish leaders and let Pilate off lightly. Other accounts of Pilate present him as a corrupt and brutal thug who would not have hesitated to kill anyone threatening public order.

Many people had reason to want Jesus dead. Christian devotion says that our sins were responsible for Jesus' death. Certainly, the same mixture of fixed ideas, desire for security, resistance to God's love and possibilities, expediency, and brutality that we find in ourselves were at work in Jesus' death.

22. WHAT IS THE MEANING OF JESUS' DEATH?

WAS GOD ANGRY?

It is sometimes said that God was angry with human beings for their sins, and that Jesus died to placate God's anger.

The Scriptures, however, emphasize God's love: "For God so loved the world that he gave his only Son" (John 3:16).

Jesus did die for our sins. He joined us in a world where sin works destructively in personal and public life. He died to save us from the power of sin.

Jesus shows us what God is like. Jesus was angry when people were mistreated and when God was presented as a taskmaster, not as a lover. He was angry for people and not at people. That is also true of God.

IT IS EASY TO UNDERSTAND why Jesus was killed. He seriously annoyed powerful people who saw him as a threat. For those who believed that God had saved the world through Jesus, however, it was much harder to explain why God would choose to act through Jesus' tortured execution.

The Scriptures do not give one single explanation but offer different perspectives. They first described Jesus as the just man who was faithful to God no matter what the cost. His agonizing death proved his faithfulness.

The prophecies of Isaiah also described a mysterious figure, the Servant, who represented the people in his faithfulness and his suffering. The early Christians often quoted these prophecies when describing Jesus' death. They helped demonstrate that his death was part of God's plan and that he died to save others.

They also reflected on the fact that Jesus had died at the time of Passover, the feast recalling how God had delivered Israel from Egypt. The feast involved the sacrifice of a lamb and the sprinkling of its blood on the doors of the houses.

This rich imagery illuminated Jesus' death. Just as the shedding of the blood of the lamb was central in freeing the Israelites, the shedding of Jesus' blood was the event through which we are freed. Also in Jewish worship, people's sins were taken away, and they were united with God through sacrifice. Jesus' death was seen as the perfect sacrifice that removed sins and united us perfectly with God.

When we ask why pain, suffering, and death should be part of God's plan, our thoughts can easily turn toward the negative. We naturally associate pain with punishment. When our parents were displeased with us, we felt unhappy. So we think that if Jesus suffered, God must have been angry with him—or with us.

The early Christians disagreed. They insisted that Jesus' suffering and death expressed God's great love. God loves us so deeply that he joins us and takes on our pain and abandonment. That is why the cross so often hangs in hospital wards. It expresses that God is with us and with all the suffering and oppressed in the world.

Jesus' followers never looked at his death in isolation. They only felt the need to explain it because they knew that he had risen from the dead. His resurrection made his cruel death puzzling.

23. JESUS' RESURRECTION

AFTER JESUS WAS CRUCIFIED, his disciples must have believed that their hopes in him were misplaced. He had said that God's kingdom was about to come through his preaching and that everything would be changed. The powerful forces in the world had taken him on, knocked him off contemptuously, and spat him out. God had done nothing; nothing had changed.

Then Jesus rose from the dead and appeared to his disciples. They believed that this was how God had intervened in the world. So they looked back on Jesus' life and his savage death in a new way. It was as if someone had promised to bring electricity to a town, had brought wiring, built substations, and then turned on the switch. When nothing happened, he was kicked out of town as a charlatan. But next evening, the lights came on and everything changed.

So at the heart of Christian faith was the conviction that Jesus had been raised from the dead. God had proved faithful to the promises, which Jesus had made in God's name. The resurrection was God's action and the beginning of God's kingdom.

None of the Gospels describe Jesus being raised to life. How it happened remained a mystery, as we

COULD JESUS' RESURRECTION BE PHOTOGRAPHED?

Of course, there were no cameras in Jesus' time. But the question invites us to ask what happened in the resurrection.

The Gospels do not describe Jesus actually rising from the dead, only his appearances to his disciples and the empty tomb. Jesus' rising is an act of God. It invites us to faith and not to speculation about how it happened.

When Jesus is raised, it is the real Jesus who is seen and not simply a ghost or a vision. He is raised bodily, but into a different dimension of bodily reality. We would need faith even to see what was in a photo.

should expect. God's action is always more than we can understand, but his resurrection had effects that we can see. The Gospels describe its consequences in two ways.

Three of the Gospels describe Jesus' appearances to his disciples. Paul also tells of other appearances. The appearances are not straightforward: Jesus appears in locked rooms. Sometimes he is not recognized until he makes himself known. The Gospels also insist that the appearances are not simply dreams. Jesus eats with his disciples to show his body is real, and invites Thomas to put his fingers into the wounds to prove he has risen.

The Gospels also describe people finding the tomb empty. In Mark's Gospel, angels are waiting for the women at the tomb. The angels, who symbolize God's mysterious action for human beings, tell the women that Christ is risen. Their message shows that God has been active in raising Jesus to life and so changing our world. The empty tomb speaks of the absence of Jesus; faith sees in it Christ's presence and victory.

24. WHAT DOES JESUS' RESURRECTION MEAN?

THE BEST WAY TO understand the meaning of the resurrection is to imagine ourselves in the story. Imagine that you are told that your dearest friend has died. You go to bed devastated and inconsolable. But you discover that she is alive when she comes to visit you the next morning. Your joy, relief, and happiness to be in her company are overwhelming. The resurrection is like that.

For the followers of Jesus, the change from the shock and desolation of the crucifixion to the joy of the resurrection was extraordinary. They had known him as their friend and teacher, and they trusted his message that God's rule would come through him. When he was brutally killed, they lost their best friend and their hopes were crushed. Then he came back to them, not as a mangled corpse, but as a person living in a free and happy state. They knew that God's kingdom had begun.

Jesus' rising from the dead changed the disciples' lives in many

RESURRECTION IN LIFE

I first met Chloe in a home for unmarried mothers. She was 15, had been abused, and was suicidal. She also had a deep faith. She gave up her baby for adoption—unmarried mothers then received no support.

I met her later in a psychiatric hospital. She had borne another child, which had been taken into care. She suffered from depression and addiction, but her faith was strong and she was determined to win back her little boy.

She did so after a hard struggle in which she felt close to Jesus in his passion. She cared well for her son for some happy years before dying young of a heart attack. Was her life wasted? No. Throughout her life, she had suffered with Christ and, in her last years, had glimpsed what it meant to rise with him.

ways. They saw that Jesus had died and risen to a full and free life. They had been touched by the hope that he had in God's power and presence in him. They had seen in his cruel death only God's absence and his own helplessness as his life ebbed away.

Now they knew God's power as they saw Jesus present with them. They saw that he was victorious over death and over the evil that had been involved in his crucifixion. They had hoped in Jesus and had despaired of him and for themselves. Now they were confident that God would transform their lives and world as God had raised Jesus to life.

Jesus had called the Twelve as proud representatives of Israel. After he was killed, they were helpless and isolated. When he rose, he called them together. The stories describe them eating, meeting, and fishing when Jesus comes to join them.

In the Gospels, the stories of Jesus rising from the dead offer us various images of what Jesus' rising from the dead means. It has many aspects, but in all of them, there is a full weighing of the hard realities that make for despair and the unexpected joy that God's love and power are greater than death, wickedness, and despair.

25. WHAT DOES JESUS' ASCENSION INTO HEAVEN MEAN?

WHEN WE THINK OF JESUS' ascension into heaven, it is hard to get beyond the technology. For us, airplanes, rockets, and space capsules make travel into the heavens a normal part of life. The stories of Jesus' ascension address very different questions that take us beyond technology.

The early Christians, who believed that with Jesus' rising, God was with them and that everything had changed, soon found themselves in hard times. They were persecuted and isolated. They wondered where Jesus had gone, and where he was now that they needed him.

The story of Jesus' ascension into heaven addresses this longing and sadness through the image of a journey. The heavens were seen as God's place. When Jesus is described as going there, it shows that he is with God. He is not far away but can help us because he is with God.

In the Acts of the Apostles, the ascension takes place just before the sending of the Spirit at Pentecost. The Spirit was Christ's Spirit, which makes Christ present to people when he is

> **THE HOLY SPIRIT AND JESUS**
>
> In the Scriptures, the Spirit of God refers to God's activity in the world. The Spirit comes upon the prophets who speak God's words, upon kings for their rule, and upon people who do God's work. God's promised rule was described as the pouring out of the Spirit.
>
> The coming of the Spirit at Pentecost was the beginning of the spread of the gospel through the Church, giving courage and good words. And the Spirit guides Paul to spread the gospel outside of the Jewish world.
>
> Paul emphasizes that the Spirit is the Spirit of Christ. The Spirit makes the risen Christ present, enabling us to live lives like Christ and to pray.

remembered in the preaching of the good news and in the prayer life of the community. The Spirit has Jesus' face and gives energy and life to the community. By the power of the Spirit, Jesus is a living and active presence in the world.

That is why Luke's story of Jesus finishes with two angels, whose role is to speak for God, telling the disciples not to look up to heaven for Jesus. He will be present and active in their community. Their business is to go back to their own world in Jerusalem where the Spirit will give them all they need to spread faith in the risen Jesus.

The story of Jesus' ascension into heaven also reminds the early Christians that, although God's promises have begun to be fulfilled in Jesus, their complete fulfillment will take place only when Jesus comes again at the end of time. So we need to reckon with Jesus' apparent absence from us, confident in our faith that he is really with us and will come again.

Jesus' ascension is a story of Jesus going away from us, but it is also a story of our going with Jesus to God. We are invited into the life of God, drawn by the power of the Spirit to accompany Jesus to the Father.

26. WHAT DOES IT MEAN TO SAY THAT JESUS SAVES US?

MANY PEOPLE FIND the saying that Jesus saves us quite quaint. It reminds them of the shaggy street preacher who asks us if we have been saved and tells us that the end is near. He makes it seem as though salvation is about individual souls going to heaven or hell depending on whether or not they believe in Jesus.

Salvation is much more than that. It says that God's promises are fulfilled in Jesus, who makes all the difference to all humanity. These promises are caught in images of freedom, light, life, plenty, healing, peace, and happiness. We can imagine what salvation means best through the story of Jesus' resurrection, when death and despair gave way to exultant life.

In the Scriptures, too, salvation is about more than my individual faith in Jesus and the eternal happiness that rewards my faith. God made promises to a nation. The people will be God's people; God will rule among them; God's kingdom will be one of peace

JESUS MEANS FREEDOM

Salvation is all about freedom. Whether trapped in our own lives or oppressed by tyrannical governments, we long for God to set us free.

Christians, who are exploited and enslaved, often pray deeply for freedom. In such songs as "Free at Last" and "Let My People Go," slaves expressed movingly their passion for freedom. They bore with their humiliation, hoping to rise with Jesus.

Like the slaves, the oppressed poor in Latin America also looked for liberation. They also found inspiration in the story of Moses, who led the Israelites out of slavery in Egypt. They knew that salvation was not simply in the next world but also touches this world.

and happiness. The Church, in which Jesus is present, is the seed that will flower in the salvation of the whole world.

The promises Jesus fulfills were not simply for the next life. They were made to a people in exile and under enemy rule. They touched this world. Furthermore, Jesus did not leave his body behind when he went to God. He rose bodily and promised us that we would rise with him in a transformed world. God is beginning his salvation of the world now through Jesus and will make it complete at the end of time.

The Scriptures offer us many images to help us grasp what salvation means. They are "before and after" images. We were slaves and then Jesus ransomed us by his death. We were exiles who then found a home. We died to sin and rose with Christ. We have passed from darkness, sorrow, and ignorance to light, joy, and knowledge. All these images point to the difference that God makes through Jesus.

The Scriptures also suggest the different ways in which Jesus has changed our lives and the world:

> He overcame the effects of Adam's disobedience through his obedience;
> His example shows us how to live holy lives; and
> His sacrifice reconciled us with God.

There are many images. Because Jesus makes all the difference, no single image will be enough.

27. WHY DID PEOPLE GATHER TOGETHER AFTER JESUS' RESURRECTION?

THE SCRIPTURES DESCRIBE the disciples fleeing in disillusion after Jesus was killed. That was natural because the life and happiness that Jesus had promised would come about through his preaching did not come. Instead they were overwhelmed by death, sadness, and disappointment. They were on their own.

Then they realized that Jesus had risen from the dead, either by meeting him or hearing through others. It was natural for them to come together again because they experienced great joy and found support in one another's company.

In the Acts of the Apostles, the building of the Christian community is shown through simple pictures. They gather to pray, at first in the synagogues and later in homes and churches. In their prayer, they remember Jesus and pray to God as Father through him. They cannot think of God without thinking of Jesus. They also support one another, having a special care for the most needy, and try to live generously and to be whole-hearted in their faith.

ONE CHURCH, MANY CHURCHES

In the early Church, the gospel spread first throughout Palestine and then throughout the Roman world. Evangelists like Paul founded local churches with their leaders, and then went on to other towns. Each church was distinctive.

But Christians also belonged to the one Church of Christ. Christ was with them making one Church out of many different peoples and nations. There was one faith, one baptism, and one hope, based in one Gospel of the one Jesus Christ.

The letters of evangelists like Paul, the visits of evangelists, prophets, and traveling Christians also strengthened this unity of faith. They encouraged and unified the churches in their faith.

It was also natural for them to gather because the promises God had made were made for the whole people. They recognized that Jesus' rising had fulfilled these promises and that God was now acting through their community to bring the good news of Jesus to the world. God called them to show through their life what it means to be saved.

The early churches were convinced that Jesus Christ was active in their own lives and had given them life and energy. They remembered Jesus through retelling the story of how God's kingdom had come through his death and resurrection as well as by breaking bread and blessing wine in the Eucharist. However, this was not simply a memory of something past; Jesus was with them in the remembering.

The faith of the early Christians was soon tested by opposition and persecution. Christ's death and rising became very real to them as they saw other Christians tortured and killed for their faith. They recognized the power of Christ's Spirit in the courage of the martyrs. They also saw how it attracted people to believe in Christ and to join the Christian community.

28. JEWS AND CHRISTIANS

IT IS EASY TO SEE THE RELATIONS between the early Christians and the Jewish people through the lens of our later history. We are familiar with the appalling history of the persecution of the Jews in Christian kingdoms and the prejudice against Jews that culminated in the Holocaust. So when we read in the Gospels of Jesus' debates with the Pharisees and the references to "the Jews" in the Fourth Gospel, we imagine that Christians and Jews were always clearly separate and hostile to one another.

That is a mistake. Jesus himself was a Jew. He went to the temple and preached in the synagogue. Jesus' followers during his life and after he rose from the dead were also Jews who went to the temple, prayed in the synagogues, followed the Mosaic Law, and believed in the promises God had made to the Jewish people. They believed that the Jewish leaders, not the people, had Jesus put to death.

After Jesus rose, his followers formed a distinctive group among the Jews. They believed that God's promises had been fulfilled in Jesus' death and rising. Jesus was the key to reading the Scriptures and following God's way. This naturally created tension with other Jews who thought this belief was wrong and blasphemous.

The pressure on both groups was heightened by events and outside forces. The Romans took reprisals for Jewish revolt, and destroyed Jerusalem and its temple. Jews outside of Palestine were also persecuted. Christian groups naturally dissociated themselves from Jews, and many Jews began to define their own identity in a way that excluded Christians.

At the same time, Christians like Paul recognized that the good news of Jesus Christ was for the whole world and not simply for the Jewish people. Those who believed in him did not have to be circumcised or to follow Jewish food laws and customs.

The stories of Jesus in the Gospels reflect this tense situation that led to the separation of the two communities. It then became easy for later Christian readers to find justification for their prejudice against Jews in the stories of the Gospels. They believed

THE DESTRUCTION OF JERUSALEM

The destruction of Jerusalem in 70 CE followed tension and revolt. After rumors that Roman officials had ransacked the temple, armed Jewish bands drove the Romans out of Jerusalem and killed many. The Roman legion that was called in was massacred at Jaffa. The Romans then sent in their army, besieged the city, destroyed the temple, and left the city as rubble. Over a million Jews were said to have died; others fled from Palestine.

The temple was the focus of Jewish worship, national life, and governance. Afterward, they united around the Law of Moses as interpreted by the rabbis. The division between Jews and Christians also became entrenched.

that Christians had replaced the Jews as God's chosen people, and that the Jews were cursed because they had killed Jesus.

These views were contrary to those of St. Paul. He believed that the promises that God made to Israel could never be revoked. They remained God's people because God was faithful, and they would also be saved.

29. HOW DID FAITH IN JESUS MOVE BEYOND THE JEWISH WORLD?

THE BIGGEST QUESTION facing the early Christians was whether you had to be a Jew to believe in Jesus or whether people from other religious backgrounds could also come to faith in Christ and join his followers. Were God's promises for the whole world or only for the Jewish people?

This question had already arisen from time to time in the Hebrew Scriptures in stories where God was shown to work for people who were not Jewish. Anyone who believes that God loved and chose one people to be his own has to ask whether that choice meant God was excluding others from the promises he made to them.

In his own ministry, Jesus often condemns the narrowness of his opponents. They held to a God whose promises apply only to the virtuous and to those faithful to the Mosaic Law. Jesus loves all and invites them to believe in God's kingdom.

After Jesus' resurrection, the question soon came to a head. People from other backgrounds came to believe in Christ. So the apostles had to decide whether to baptize them and accept them into the Church, and if so, whether they had to be circumcised and follow the details of the Jewish law in eating and washing and so on. This would make it very difficult to preach faith in Christ to those who were not Jews.

Paul pushed the question hard. He was a devout Jew who believed that God's promises applied only to those who were devout in their Jewish observance. When he came to believe in Christ, he found a God who saved through Jesus' execution as a criminal. The God whom Paul knew had reconciled the whole world to himself and had set people free from anxiety about obeying the law in detail. The good news of Jesus was for all people.

After strong debate between the leaders of the early Church, Paul was appointed to preach the Gospel to non-Jews and to gather them into local churches. The Acts of the Apostles describes him going from meeting the apostles in Jerusalem, the spiritual center of the Jews, to preaching the Gospel through Syria, Asia Minor, Greece, and finally going as a captive to Rome, the capital of the Roman Empire. Faith in Christ had gone global, but conflict continued between the followers of Jesus who insisted that everyone follow the Jewish law and those, such as Paul, who insisted that they be free of obligation.

Accepting people from non-Jewish backgrounds into the Church created a challenge for Christians. To understand what God had done through Jesus, they also needed to know about God's promises to Israel and how Jesus had fulfilled them. So they needed to be introduced to the wonderful stories of the rescue from Egypt, of the prophets and the exile, and of God's faithfulness to his people.

As they came to know more of Jewish life, they became more attracted to it, and some identified with both communities. The Christian teachers then had to make God's action for Israel part of their lives and, at the same time, insist that faith in Christ had to be lived within the Christian community. This sometimes led them to attack contemporary Jewish faith and its life in ways that were harsh and unacceptable.

> ### THE COUNCIL OF JERUSALEM
>
> The Acts of the Apostles describes a crucial meeting of the apostles in Jerusalem in about 50 CE. The key issue was whether non-Jewish converts to Christ should have to be circumcised. The apostles required only that non-Jewish converts should abstain from meat sacrificed to idols and some other meats and unchastity. Paul, whose mission was to non-Jews, did not insist on these dietary rules.
>
> The decision of the council made the mission to non-Jews possible. However, it also created strong tension with the continuing Jewish community, which emphasized the importance of circumcision. It also created a distinction between Jewish Christians who followed the Law and non-Jewish converts who did not.

30. HOW WAS CHRIST BROUGHT TO OTHER CULTURES?

AS FAITH IN CHRIST spread, Christian preachers faced a challenge: how to speak of what God had done in Jesus in ways that their hearers would understand. The language of the Scriptures was often hard to enter for people brought up on other stories and in other religious traditions. Thus, preachers had to find connections between their hearers' background and the Gospel of Jesus.

When people speak across cultures, whether as migrants entering a new culture or as people attracted to a new faith, there is always two-way change. The person is changed by the message they hear. And the message is changed, as people understand it in their own way. The challenge is to ensure that the heart of the message is not changed, but seen in new and richer ways.

The early Christians had to speak of Christ to different audiences. The people who

---

PAUL AT THE AREOPAGUS (ACTS OF THE APOSTLES 17:22–34)

Paul once addressed an educated Greek audience. In Athens, he was provoked by the number of idols he saw and criticized them. He was brought up to the Areopagus, the center of public life in Athens, to explain himself.

He did not use scriptural language, but rather referred to a nearby altar to an unknown god to commend in words familiar to his educated hearers the God whom Christians knew. Many of them would have seen images of the gods as symbols. Finally, he spoke of the coming judgment and of Jesus whom God had raised from the dead.

The mention of the resurrection stopped his hearers short. Some found it absurd; others were polite. Educated Romans could not grasp this central point in Christian faith.

were attracted to Christ in the Roman world often saw religion as something that was done in society. Sacrifice to different gods was common, as was sacrifice to the emperor. There were many gods, and on one occasion, even Paul was worshipped as a god. Thus, Jesus could easily be seen as a god. The challenge was to show people that there was only one God, the Father of Jesus Christ.

Christians also soon had to find a way of speaking of Christ to Roman officials who declared their faith to be illegal. Some spoke of Jesus as a philosopher who taught the true way of living. Their challenge was then to explain why their Roman authorities had executed him.

Educated Romans also heard of the God of Jesus Christ. Paul met them in Athens and explained the connections between Christian faith and the ideas of Greek philosophers and writers, but they found incredible his assertion that Jesus had been raised bodily from the dead. His hearers believed that happiness lay in being freed from the body, not in being reunited with it after death.

In all of these conversations, Jesus came to have a different face, as he does today. Most Western painters gave Jesus a European face, which is what we have become most familiar with, but he also has an Indian, an Australian Indigenous, an African, and a Chinese face. The stories of Jesus are told in many languages, and each culture finds new insights and new possibilities in the story of Jesus.

31. JESUS, SON OF GOD

THE RISEN JESUS was at the center of the early Christians' faith. They believed that through Jesus' resurrection, God had fulfilled the promises he made to Israel, and that Jesus was present with them through God's Spirit. They understood that the way to know God was through Jesus' life and death. They made their prayers to God through Jesus, and they prayed to Jesus himself, saying "Come Lord Jesus." They could not speak about God without speaking of Jesus.

This was also reflected in the names they gave Jesus. These all stressed the closeness of Jesus to God. They called him the *image of God* and the *Word* (meaning "mind" or "reason") of God. They addressed Jesus as *Lord*, the name Jews reserved to God alone. They also called him the *Son of God*.

This became a favorite way to describe Jesus. It indicated the closeness between God and Jesus—Jesus was "family." The Christians referred to God as their "Father." It also suggested Jesus' faithfulness in doing what God wanted of him. It indicated

THE COUNCIL OF NICAEA

The debate about Jesus' relationship to God became acute after the Roman emperors stopped persecuting Christianity. Because Christians and their ideas could now travel freely, debate spread widely and became an issue for the empire as well as the Church.

The emperor called the bishops to Nicaea, funded their travel, and asked them to compose a statement of faith for all to sign. This became a precedent for resolving later conflicts, but it also raised questions about the relationship between the emperor and the Church.

The creed to which Christians were asked to assent included an unscriptural phrase with an ambiguous history. Many bishops who rejected Arius's ideas also deplored the reference to "substance." As a result, the debate continued after Arius died.

the importance of Jesus in God's plan, and it linked Jesus to us—if Jesus was Son, we who were joined to him were also God's children.

By associating God and Jesus so closely, Christians faced great criticism. They were accused of making Jesus into a second God, thus betraying the core Jewish belief that there is only one God and no other.

They insisted that God was one. To explain how God might be one but also Father and Son, they used images like the relationship between a human being and her mind, or between the source of light and its brightness. The relationship between God and Christ was inseparable and existed from eternity.

They were eventually pushed to speak more definitely about Jesus when Arius, a priest from Egypt, claimed that Jesus was at the center of God's plans for humanity, but was created by God. In the conflict that followed, it became clear that many scriptural passages could be construed in this direction. The deeper question was about what the whole message of Christ demanded. Christians recognized that the good news of Jesus Christ consisted in the Son of God entering our world and dying for us in Jesus. They recognized that whatever God is, Jesus is. They differ only in being Father and Son.

32. JESUS AND THE TRINITY

CHRISTIANS SOMETIMES SPEAK of God as the Trinity, in which Jesus is the Second Person, together with the Father and the Son. The New Testament does not speak of the Trinity. So how did Jesus come to be associated with the Trinity?

The seeds of an answer can be seen in the New Testament where Jesus speaks to God intimately as Father in the same way as we do. Paul also speaks of God as the Father of Jesus Christ. So Jesus has a special relationship with God as Father, but *Jesus* is not just another name for God.

The Scriptures also speak of the coming of the Spirit of God, who makes Christ present to us. We cannot speak of God without speaking of Christ and the Spirit. However, they are not identical because Jesus promises that the Father will send the Spirit after his rising from the dead.

So in the Christian faith, Father, Son, and the Spirit are all divine, but God, as the Jews and Jesus himself insisted, was one God.

> **THE LIVING GOD**
>
> For some people, their faith in the Trinity changes their whole lives. Fr. Louis Robert, a French Canadian who spent much of his life in Vietnam and in the Vietnamese refugee camps in Asia, was like that.
>
> He was a forceful, craggy-faced man, untiring in his care and advocacy for his people. When he spoke of the Trinity, however, his voice and face changed. He became lost in the mystery of God and of the wonder of God's life as Father, Son, and Holy Spirit. His faith was not a matter of the right words or thoughts, but it took over his whole being.

The early Christians did not try to speak precisely about the relationship between Father, Son, and Holy Spirit. When Arius denied that Christ was fully God, he forced them to think more seriously about how God could be Father, Son, and Spirit but, at the same time, one God.

As they came to realize that the Gospel depended on God coming in his own self to join us, they had to ask how God could be one and undivided if Christ were fully divine in the same way as the Father. They said that both these things must be true.

This led others to ask if the Spirit, too, is also fully divine or is created—an angel. They realized also that the Spirit was not a messenger, but was God's own self. When the Spirit prays within us, it is God who prays within us.

Still, they insisted that there was only one God, who existed as Father, Son, and Holy Spirit. They did not explain how this could be, but they saw that when Jesus made us one with God, he was drawing us into the life of God. The Spirit draws us to Jesus who brings us with him to the Father. When we pray through Christ to the Father, it is the Spirit within us who prays. The Trinity is not about numbers, but about the inner life of God.

33. JESUS, GOD AND MAN

THE DEBATE ABOUT Jesus' relationship to God affected the way in which people saw him. Christians, who defended Jesus' full divinity, emphasized his divinity and his difference from ordinary human beings. God was strong and human beings weak; God was all knowing and all powerful, whereas human beings were ignorant. We can see this tendency in the prayers of the time. The risk in this view was that God and human beings could be seen as opposites. When that happens, it becomes hard to see how Jesus can be both God and human.

To put it crudely, either Jesus' divinity would blow his humanity away as a lightning strike does to a computer, or Jesus' divinity would have to be toned down to be accommodated in his humanity. Or Jesus would be a sandwich being, in

THE EASTERN CHURCHES

The statement by the Council of Chalcedon, that the one Christ was fully God and fully human, did not heal division. Bishops associated with Antioch had already fled to Persia. Many bishops associated with Egypt rejected Chalcedon. Emperors vacillated as they tried to secure unity.

Ultimately, only churches associated with Constantinople and with Rome accepted Chalcedon. The Nestorian Churches, named after the Antiochene leader, spread outside of the Roman Empire through Persia and into China. The Monophysite Churches, named after their belief in the one nature of Christ, spread through Egypt and Syria, influencing the church in Ethiopia.

These churches are a precious part of Christianity. They have been devastated after recent Western military interference in the Middle East and the reaction to it by Muslim groups.

which his humanity and divinity each occupy its own space, but they are not really united in Jesus Christ.

In all these ways of imagining the relationship between Jesus' divinity and humanity, the unique heart of the Christian faith in Jesus is lost. God's promises were fulfilled when he loved human beings so deeply that he sent his Son to come among us and unite us to himself. This implied that Jesus was not only God and human, but also brought together divinity and humanity in himself.

How this could be so was debated heatedly within the Church. As so often happens in church disputes, people used the same words with different meanings and were horrified at what their opponents said. They had to find an agreed-upon language.

They did this by setting out the essential things that needed to be said about Jesus: that he was fully divine and fully human, that he had a human mind and inner life, and that he was one being and not God and a man stuck together. They then spoke of his humanity and divinity as two natures and asserted that he was one being by saying that he was one person.

They did not offer a recipe to describe how God was truly God and truly human; they simply set out to protect the core of faith in Jesus Christ.

34. WHAT DOES THE INCARNATION MEAN?

THE HEART OF CHRISTIAN faith lies in God's relationship to human beings. God called them into being, chose Israel as his people, and rescued them from slavery in Egypt. The same God sent his Son to join human beings. Christ died for them and rose to unite them with God.

The Christian imagination was caught by God taking on our humanity so that he could share with us his divinity. People meditated deeply on the line from the Fourth Gospel, "The Word became flesh and lived among us" (John 1:14). By sharing our death, he shared with us his risen life. This uniting of divine and human in Christ is called the *incarnation*—the coming into flesh of the Son of God.

This summed up the heart of Christian faith and was spelled out delicately in Christian art and hymns. We find it expressed most appealingly in Christmas carols that play with the contrast between the grandeur of God and the messiness of the human life that the Son of God lived. The maker of the stars was revealed to the Magi by a star; the all-powerful God lay dependent in the manger; the first people invited to the court of the King of the world were dirty, smelly shepherds.

This image of Jesus has colored in different ways the perspective from which Christians look at the world. Some people stress the way in which the coming of Christ has blessed and transformed our world in Christ. The ordinary things of the world are made holy because he has touched them. They emphasize the holiness of the Church, the sacredness of the Mass and of liturgical celebrations, and the reverence that should be found in liturgical music and given to the chalice and plate used in the Eucharist. By coming into the world, God sets apart what he touches.

Others emphasize the dignity and the preciousness of the world and of humanity that God has joined. All that God has made is good and reflects his beauty and glory.

SEEING CHRIST IN OTHERS

Early Christian stories often describe Christ appearing as a beggar. St. Christopher agrees to carry a beggar across the river, for example, only to discover that the beggar was Jesus.

St. Benedict tells his monks that when guests come, it is Christ who comes. He echoes Jesus' saying that those who visit the sick and imprisoned visit him.

This does not mean that we should imagine other people as Jesus, but that we are the Body of Christ and so joined to all our brothers and sisters in him.

It is a challenge to see and welcome Christ in people who may be ungrateful and disreputable. However, these are the people loved and for whom Jesus died.

Human beings must have a deep value if the Son of God can come into a human life and be united with us.

So when we think of the Incarnation, we are awakened to the beauty, delicacy, and preciousness of every being in our world. In our faith, the ordinary things in which Christ comes to us—the water of baptism, the bread and wine of the Eucharist, the love between husband and wife, and the oil poured on the sick—are not ordinary at all. They can bear the Son of God to us. So we should respect and love the ordinary things of the world because nothing that God has made is ordinary.

These are two different ways of reflecting on the Incarnation, and both convey part of what Jesus means for us.

PART THREE

Why Does Jesus Matter?

35. WHY DOES JESUS MATTER TODAY?

FOR MANY PEOPLE today, Jesus doesn't matter at all. Some live in nations with other religious traditions or have been raised without any knowledge of Jesus. Others were brought up Christian but now find it irrelevant to their lives.

For other people, Jesus is important, but for many different reasons. Some are interested in him because he has been such a central figure in Western culture and in world history. If we don't know anything about Jesus, centuries of Western art will be less meaningful. We will also miss the point of much Western literature and ignore a central strand in the development of Western institutions. From this perspective, knowledge of Jesus is important for any well-educated person.

Some people are fascinated by the stories of Jesus and believe they have much to say to the contemporary world. However, they find much that is unbelievable. So they retell the story in ways they think inspiring and acceptable. They might leave out, for example, any mention of a life after death, of Christ's divinity, and of his resurrection. Jesus remains important to them as a moral teacher with a lesson for humanity.

> ## THE MUSLIM JESUS
>
> In Islam, Jesus matters. He is seen as a prophet and miracle worker, born by God's will from Mary, who is also held in great respect. He did not die on the cross but was taken into heaven.
>
> Jesus is honored as the last prophet to the Jewish people and the Messiah, who prepared the way for Muhammad, the last and decisive prophet to whom the Qur'an was given.
>
> Jesus will return before the last days, but not as a prophet, to defeat the Antichrist. Seen through Muslim eyes, Jesus is greatly to be honored, but he is neither the Son of God nor God's final word.

Others find Jesus important because of his message. Some emphasize his harsh criticism of the wealthy and his care for the poor or his resistance to the Jewish religious authorities, seeing him as a model for social activists. Some stress his consistent refusal to join resistance groups and the attention he gives to our relationship to God, and see him as a model for separating religion from politics.

All of these responses to Jesus can illuminate central aspects of his life and teaching, but they each represent a very limited view of the Jesus in whom the early Christians believed and whom we meet in the New Testament. They obscure the central relationship of Jesus to God and the way in which he fulfills the promises that God made to Israel.

The question we address in this third section is how the Jesus whom we meet in the New Testament and in the faith of the early Church matters today. What difference might it make to our lives and our world if we accept a Jesus like that?

36. WHY DOES THE JESUS OF CHRISTIAN FAITH MATTER TODAY?

WE SHOULD NOT TAKE for granted that, simply because we are church-going Christians, we believe in the Jesus of the New Testament. Faith in that Jesus was challenging then, and it is challenging today. It challenges our view of ourselves and of our world. However, if we do see Jesus as the early Christians did, Jesus can make a difference both to our vision of life and to the way in which we live.

BELIEF AND FAITH

In the Gospels, when Jesus praises people for their faith, he usually means that they have trusted that God is working through him.

After he rose, faith in him meant trusting that he has brought God's kingdom and living his way. Faith was an attitude of the heart that guided our hands and feet.

Of course, we only trust people if we know them. To trust in the Jesus whom we meet in the New Testament means believing that God acts through him, that he is present with us, and that we shall be raised with him.

Thus faith is a trust that fills our hearts, guides our steps, and shapes our minds.

The key to Christian faith, which makes it incredible to many of our contemporaries, is the conviction that God intervened in our world in Jesus. It involves belief in a God who made and loves each human being and the world of which we form part passionately and intimately. That God enters into a special relationship with the people of Israel and promises a world of happiness and peace. Even more than that, love drives God to fulfill these promises by entering our world in Jesus, sharing our experience, and finally dying and rising for us.

If this belief enters our bones, it will color the way we

see our world and respond to it. We will not be able to take our world for granted or accept without protest the mess we make of it. God loves it and entrusts it to us as its stewards.

Nor can we take people for granted. God loves each human being tenderly and thus invites us to be responsible to each other. Christ died between two thieves whom he also loved. He invites us to notice the way in which people who are disadvantaged in our society are treated and to respond to them.

In Jesus' rising, God has given us an image of what we and our world are made for and our possibilities if we follow Jesus' way. We live in a world that Christ has begun to transform, and we are part of its re-making.

This is a broad picture. The following points will expand on the ways in which Jesus makes a difference to us and to our world.

37. HOW DOES FAITH IN JESUS MAKE A DIFFERENCE?

IMAGINE THAT ALL we could say about Jesus was that he was a great man who died bravely and tragically. His sayings and actions lived on and inspired people like ourselves. If that were the whole story, Jesus' life would still have been a great gift to us. We might remember him and be inspired by him as people have been captured by the lives of Nelson Mandela and Dorothy Day.

The Jesus we know through Christian faith, however, is something more than that. We believe that he died, that God raised him from the dead, that he is now with us, and that he will come again. We believe that he is present with us. That makes a great difference.

In the first place, Jesus is not simply a figure in the history of our world, but is present now in our world and is working in the lives of those who believe in him. We say, "Christ has died," but also that "Christ is risen."

That Christ is present to us means that he is not simply someone whom we remember. He is a person

POPE FRANCIS SHOWS THE DIFFERENCE

Pope Francis has shown us what happens when Jesus shapes a person and how it can change the world. He does things Jesus' way—lives simply, goes to an island to grieve for people who drowned seeking a better life, washes a young Muslim woman prisoner's feet, and insists on flying through storms to a Philippine tornado-struck town. Wherever he goes, he brings the joy and the freedom of the gospel.

He urges us to allow the joy of the gospel to lead us out of our comfortable places to the edges of our world. We are not to be sourpusses telling people what they can't do, but like Jesus, giving them hope for a freer and a better way.

to whom we can pray and with whom we can have a close personal relationship. When we hear the Gospel stories of him, we can easily move from wondering what he did to talking with him. We can engage with him as someone who is present to us.

Jesus also offers us a way of living that carries authority and promises companionship. We may be inspired by a Martin Luther King Jr. or a Robert Kennedy and want to imitate their courage. However, when we look at Jesus' death and rising, we are not simply inspired by his courage. We know that his way is God's way and that he calls us to follow his path through death to life. We know that wherever our following of Jesus takes us, he will be with us and that the suffering and failure we experience share in his dying and will end in our rising with him. That is why we can see Martin Luther King's death as a victory and not as a loss.

The crucial difference that Christ's presence to us in faith makes is that he can capture our imagination and make our relationship with God like that with a lover. Our dreams, our hopes, and our memories all revolve around Jesus and the deep relationship he has with us.

38. HOW DOES JESUS CHANGE THE WAY WE SEE THE WORLD?

WE CAN SEE THE WORLD in many different ways. Some people don't think about it at all; they simply take it for granted and get on with their lives in it. For others, it began with the big bang and is now cooling down; they prefer not to think about it. Some see it as a miserable place where we can expect pain and suffering and survive best by not having high hopes.

If these are our natural ways of seeing the world, Jesus does make a difference to them. The story of Jesus tells us that God loves the world and people in it deeply and passionately. God's beauty is reflected in the beauty of the world. God's love is shown by God's Son wanting to join the world, live a human life in it, and die to save the world. Part of that salvation involves reconciling people to the world so that we do not simply use and exploit it, but respect it as God's place given to all human beings as a precious gift.

If we believe that God calls us to follow Jesus too, we recognize that we need to take the world seriously. It is the place God invites us to care for and to respect. Our faith is not simply in our head or our heart, but in our hands and feet, in our working together to make a just and hospitable world, in our walking with people who are broken and isolated, in touching the lonely and abandoned. To be part of the world to which Jesus came is necessarily to take it seriously.

The story of Jesus also reminds us that we have mistreated and damaged our world. The end of Jesus' life was a tortured death in which a tree, one of the beautiful things of our world, was hacked down so a human being could be nailed to it. The story of our world is not simply one of beauty and love, but of horror, ugliness, sin, greed, and failure. Instead of being the table at which all people can sit and eat, it has been exploited for the good of a few. In Jesus, we see the shame of the way in which the natural world and human beings are treated. We cannot simply shrug our shoulders and move on.

Jesus also suggests that our hopes for the world and for humanity are higher. His rising allows us to hope that our world will be transformed and we with it. The beauty and the preciousness we see from a mountain top or the new growth on a spring morning are not simply a diversion from a harsh and unfeeling reality. They are an image of the world that God loves and in Jesus will transform.

CHRIST IN ART

People have long argued whether we should portray God and holy people in art. The Jewish tradition has been very strongly against it, as later has been the Islamic tradition. Some Christian groups have also regarded images of God, Christ, and the saints as idolatry.

Catholics believe that images of Christ and the saints help us to pray and to know Sacred Scripture. Just as Christ is the true image of God and human beings are made in God's image, so images of Christ help us to worship.

Because Christ is the image of God, we should also respect artists whose images can help us find God in the beauty, variety, and terror of our world.

39. HOW CAN JESUS' PRESENCE IN THE CHURCH MAKE A DIFFERENCE?

FOR MANY PEOPLE, churches are strange places — they seem archaic and bound up with the past. It is as if people who were deeply affected by the story of the Greek philosopher, Plato, built a museum to which they came each week to talk about his philosophy and be inspired by him to live reflectively. Many people who saw them would tell them to forget the past and focus on living in the contemporary world.

If we believe in the Jesus whom the early Christians knew, we see things quite differently. The Church is not simply a gathering of people who remember a Jesus now dead. Jesus is present bringing and holding them together. It is like the difference between a heater when the power is switched on and when it is switched off. The Spirit of Jesus is like the electricity that brings the heater to life by providing warmth.

In the church community, Christ gives energy and spirit to the people who form the church, makes a community out of a collection of individuals, invites people to follow him, heals those who are sick in spirit, and draws the community out to

ECUMENISM

The early followers of Jesus saw themselves as the community of people whom Jesus had saved. Their unity with one another was a symbol of God's unity with humanity.

So a divided Church betrayed what Christ was about. They would see the present division of the Church into denominations as a scandal.

Catholics believe that the Church in its fullness exists in the Roman Catholic Church, but other Christian churches share in the reality of the Church through baptism, preaching, and following Jesus. We all must pray and work to make the Church visibly one as Christ wants.

those who are at the margins. Christ makes the life of the Church a seed of the kingdom of God, which he brings. The heart of the Church is Christ.

One of St. Paul's favorite ways of describing the Church is as the Body of Christ. We are joined to Christ by dying to sin with him. We share the life he promises in rising from the dead and in the coming of his kingdom. The widow and the wino, the executive and the prisoner awaiting execution, the straight and the gay come together as members of the Body of Christ.

Christ is also in the Church reconciling us to God and to one another. This happens in the simple meeting of people as a community. In the Church, we do not choose our companions. We come from different postcodes, different nations, and different social groups. We are brought together by the story of Jesus, by our following of Jesus, and in our attempt to follow him in living by his gospel.

Jesus also says that reconciliation is more than strangers getting on in the local congregation. The life we try to shape together is the seed of a reconciled world. The peace, the desire to listen and not shout, to make peace and not war, and to build courage and not scramble for security show the path to a wider reconciliation in our world.

40. HOW MIGHT JESUS' PRESENCE IN THE SACRAMENTS MAKE A DIFFERENCE?

IMAGINE THAT THE CHURCH were completely computerized. When a baby is brought to the church for the first time, she or he would be given a number, password, and entered into the data base; marriages would simply be entered in the same way, and an electronic postcard would be sent to the couple; instead of church services, a sermon would be e-mailed to subscribers; at death, our files would simply be moved from the current file to the archives.

To our way of thinking, this computerized Church might seem very impersonal. The reason why has to do with Jesus. The heart of Christian life is personal. Its key moments are when people meet and when they engage with their world. Faith in Jesus comes in things: Christ meets us in our day-to-day world. We

> ## SEVEN SACRAMENTS
>
> For Catholics, there are seven sacraments: baptism, confirmation, reconciliation, Eucharist, holy orders, marriage, and anointing of the sick.
>
> The seven sacraments are part of a larger story. In Jesus, God comes into our world and invites us to find God in the friendships, illnesses, meals, work, and messiness of our daily lives.
>
> Some activities became part of the shared life of the Church. Sick people were anointed with oil. Preachers had hands laid on them. People were immersed in water when entering the Church, and worshipped Christ through a sacred meal. Marriages and reconciliation found their own gestures.
>
> Many rituals echoed Jesus' own life, particularly baptism and Eucharist. They were called *sacraments*. Later in the life of the Church, they became more systematized and numbered. Hence, we speak of seven sacraments.

meet as the Church in our bodies and not as pure spirits. When we gather as Church, Christ is active through the people we sit near with their deafness, hacking coughs, noisy babies, and nodding off during the sermon.

Christ is also present in the events that act as signposts in our lives: at birthdays, marriage anniversaries, the beginning of school and graduation, our first day at work and our last, our first overseas journey by ourselves, the birth of our first child, and the day our last child moves out of the home. These are times when we meet God in the world he joined in Jesus.

Significant church events that remember the love that God shows us in Jesus are also "thingy." We enter the Church by having people gather around us and having water poured over our heads. We are joined to Christ, who went down into the waters of death and rose out of them.

In the event that shapes our membership of the Church, the Eucharist, Christ is with us as we eat and drink together, and we are joined to his dying and rising. If we marry, Christ is present with us in all the hesitant and loving encounters that make us into one body as we are all one body in him. When we are ill, we may have oil poured on us. Oil was used to strengthen athletes; in the same way, Christ strengthens us to recover our health or to prepare for our journey to God.

41. HOW MIGHT JESUS' PRESENCE IN THE EUCHARIST MAKE A DIFFERENCE?

IMAGINE IF THE PEOPLE who gathered to celebrate the Eucharist on Sunday were just a random group of people meeting to remember an event that took place two thousand years ago. They told a story of Jesus' last meal and just ate bread and sipped wine.

That would be a good thing to do and we may get a lot out of doing it: we might make friends when we go to church, and our coming together would help us to pray. But it would be different from what our faith in Jesus makes us do at the Eucharist. The Spirit makes Jesus present in all these things. We engage with him as someone present, not simply as someone remembered.

In the Eucharist, Jesus is not there as something to be worshipped. He is present as someone active. When we remember what he did in the Last Supper, he is there with us giving himself to God. We join with

SACRIFICE AND MEAL

During the Last Supper, Jesus ate with his disciples and told them to do what he did. Mark, Matthew, and Luke describe it as a Passover meal, which would have included bread, herbs, meat, and wine. Thus, we call the Eucharist a meal.

The Jewish meal was ritualized: prayers of thanksgiving accompanied cups of wine throughout the meal.

When Jesus told his disciples to "do this in memory of me," he also referred to his life and his coming death. When we eat, we join ourselves to Jesus' offering of himself to God in his death. The Eucharist is a sacrificial meal.

In the Eucharist, Jesus is not only remembered but acts. He comes to us, feeds us, and brings us into his death and rising.

him in what he does. He also feeds us, welcomes us, and sends us out to wait for him. So our prayer at the Eucharist is not simply one of remembering. It is a prayer to someone who is there with us and whose life we share.

Jesus is also present in the Word of God that we hear. As we listen to the Gospel, we are brought into his presence and we listen to him speaking to us. We receive Jesus as the Word of God in the same way as we receive him as the Body of Christ.

When we receive the Body of Christ and drink his blood in the Eucharist, Christ feeds us and is our food. He is present in the bread and wine that are blessed. When we receive the Eucharist, we are united with him and he lives within us.

Jesus is also present to us in the people who celebrate the Eucharist and in the larger community of his followers around the world. The Church is also the Body of Christ. In the Eucharist, Christ shapes us into his body, linked by the love that he has for us and that he asks us to show to one another.

The difference between the Eucharist and a gathering in which Jesus is simply remembered is that the Spirit of God makes Jesus present to us.

42. HOW MIGHT BEING THANKFUL FOR JESUS MAKE A DIFFERENCE?

SAYING THANK YOU is a gift to others and also to ourselves. It makes us more attentive to our life and our world. If we regularly pray in thanks to God, our prayer gradually changes us. We notice the wind in the trees, the evening sunlight, and the kindness of strangers, and our life becomes a way of saying thanks.

Thanksgiving, however, is not just about sweet times and easy places. Annie worked as a nurse in an African refugee camp, caring especially for the elderly. It was a cruel place with little food. One day when Annie was feeling hopeless, an old woman came to give her two small eggs. She was bent at the waist, her body at a ninty-degree angle, and she walked supported by a branch.

She and Annie chatted until she heard music of her own country being played in the office. She stood and began to sway and dance, taking Annie's hands in her own; her eyes closed and face joyful. They danced, laughed, and embraced.

SURPRISED BY GRATITUDE

Most of us identify prayer with asking God for things. That is right—when we come to God with big desires and desperate hearts, we come to trust. That is why Jesus tells us to bombard God when praying—to be God "botherers."

Yet in the Lord's Prayer, Jesus does not begin with asking. He begins by praising God. So we can begin prayer by standing before our lives and holding them out before God.

When we wonder at God, we instinctively say thank you: for the world through which we glimpse his love and beauty, for bringing us into being, for joining us in Jesus, and for inviting to follow Jesus. Then we can be playful in prayer and deluge God with requests for the big things that we and our world need.

Annie's own heart grew full and she was overwhelmed by the goodness of God.

Thankfulness is always a gift. It gives us a context in which to set all the betrayals, mediocrity, failure, and unfaithfulness we meet from others, as well as the gap between our dreams of generosity and our selfish actions. When we know that God loves us tenderly and calls us to follow Jesus, we naturally thank God for being so compassionate to us.

We can see the difference that this gratitude to God makes when we are in the company of people who notice everything but can express only disappointment and resentment for all the slights they receive and for the messiness of the world. They do not see people's kindness, only their faults; they do not say thank you, do not bless, but continually complain and curse. Of course, we know that we are often like that as well.

To say thank you to God each day for our lives puts us into touch with God's intimate love for us, and links our celebration of the Eucharist—the great thank you to God for Christ—with the events of our day.

As gratitude becomes a habit, we become more gentle, and other people can see Jesus in our lives.

43. HOW MIGHT FOLLOWING JESUS' WAY OF LIFE MAKE A DIFFERENCE?

ALL RELIGIONS ENCOURAGE their followers to live generously and well. The Mosaic Law of the Jews is full of instructions about how to relate to our neighbor; Buddhists emphasize the importance of compassion to all living beings. You don't need to believe in Jesus Christ to be generous. Indeed, during his life, Jesus pointed to people from different religions and races as examples of generosity.

However, belief in Jesus does shape our lives in distinctive ways. As we remember the pattern of his life and the stories told about him, our lives become stitched to his. We come to see the events and encounters of our own lives through the lens of the large and the small stories of Jesus. When we meet suffering, we set it against the large story of Jesus' death and rising from the dead. We may see ourselves as suffering with Jesus and find hope in that thought.

The stories Jesus told and the lessons he taught may be seen against the daily events of our lives. When we meet a homeless person in the street whom we would not ordinarily notice, we may remember the story of

A LIVED FAITH

The anniversary Mass of a small Central American Catholic community was near, and I was gathering the names of their dead. In a small wooden hut, a gracious woman welcomed me warmly. She told me that her seven sons had died, and she named them one by one. Three were murdered because they were catechists; the others had been killed by the armed forces. She paused, as she named her youngest, Juan Luis. Tears came into her eyes as she said, "And I had such hope in him."

Her faith had sustained this quiet and unknown woman in raising and mothering her children, in grieving them, and in helping build this community.

the Good Samaritan and speak kindly to the person, and perhaps even accept their invitation to help them. As we see ourselves playing a part in Jesus' story, our way of living changes.

Similarly, when we feel that our life has turned down an alley that comes to a dead end, the story of the Prodigal Son may make us recognize our need and our separation from God's love. Our heart may be touched by the desire to live in a better way. As these stories become real to us, they do not simply affect our minds and our hearts, but begin to move our hands and feet as well.

When the stories of Jesus come alive in our imagination, we naturally develop a conversational relationship to Jesus. We talk to him about our lives, and find his words about love for our neighbor, about prayer, about God's love for us and others in our misery part of our thinking. We imagine a generous way of living in which Jesus is central, and we are encouraged to try to bring it into our lives.

Following Jesus generously begins with an imagination that is captured by his dying and rising and is fed by the stories and sayings found in the Gospels.

44. HOW MIGHT CHRIST'S COMPASSION MAKE A DIFFERENCE?

POPE FRANCIS HAS made a great impression on Catholics and on the wider world. That comes partly out of his evident compassion. He describes himself as above all a sinner on whom God has had compassion. For him, the story of Jesus is a story of compassion. It is reflected in Pope Francis's own refusal to judge people and in his joy in visiting people who, in jails and elsewhere, are often judged very harshly.

If Jesus lives in our imagination, we will constantly be forced to recognize how judgmental we so often are. We find that our responses to situations are so different from his. His example will also invite us to be compassionate. We find ourselves looking at the woman caught in adultery and the people ready to stone her, and hear Jesus saying to us, "Let anyone among you who is without sin be the first to throw a stone." Jesus may also invite us to be moved by the suffering and death of others when we see him weeping at the

---

A CHRISTMAS DAY MASS

A few days before Christmas in the 1980s, a camp on the Cambodian border was shelled. Many people were killed, and the people were evacuated to a safe but unsheltered bush site. Fr. Pierre Ceyrac, who lived as simply as the refugees, had celebrated the Mass in the camp the week before Christmas Day.

On Christmas Day, he returned to celebrate in the open air with blue plastic for the altar and a Khmer scarf as a stole. He first embraced people who had lost relatives with tears running down his cheeks, and introduced the Mass, saying, "Today is Christmas Day, and we share in the unutterable poverty of Jesus Christ." His lived faith in Jesus and the people's own faith made all the difference that day.

death of his friend Lazarus. The stories of Jesus disclose a man with a big heart. If we accept his invitation to enter the compassion of his heart, we will be taken into God's compassionate heart.

Jesus' actions and words also divert us from our addiction to big words and make us attend to people. They invite us not to condemn but to be compassionate. We do not see people as branded with a false religion, with bad moral principles, or with the mark of an inferior race.

We see their human faces, each of whom God loves passionately and invites us to go out to with compassion and hospitality. Good theology and moral principles are important. However, they do not define people or shape the way in which we should respond to them.

It is particularly important to know Jesus' compassion when we are affronted by the brutality and unfairness of the world and want to do something to change the lives of people oppressed by it. If we work with people who are marginalized, we will become marginalized ourselves. When that happens, it is easy to despair, to burn out, to feed on our anger, and become judgmental. If we are to hang in with people who are marginalized, we need Jesus' compassion for the people whom we love, for ourselves, and for those who do not see.

45. HOW MIGHT JESUS HELP US FACE DEATH AND FAILURE?

IN MANY CATHOLIC HOSPITALS, a crucifix hangs in each room. It is sometimes seen simply as part of the Catholic badging of the hospital. State-run and for-profit hospitals have pictures of the president or of the founder of the hospital in their room. Catholic hospitals have the image of Jesus on the cross. However, the cross is not simply a sign of identity. It offers a deeper perspective on the suffering and fear that we so often feel when we are seriously ill or facing tests in a hospital.

At first sight, this reminder of Jesus dying in pain may seem to be just another harsh reminder of the suffering from which we want to escape. It rubs our noses in pain. However, if Jesus' death and rising are important in our lives, the cross can be a comforting reminder that God loves us deeply and is with us in our suffering. Because Jesus has experienced all the pain, fear, resentment, turmoil, sadness, and despair that we

THE SIGN OF THE CROSS

The cross was a widespread religious symbol, but in the Roman world, it was associated with torture and execution. St. Paul saw that Jesus had conquered sin and death through his brutal death. Thus the cross became a symbol of Christian hope.

Christians soon marked it on graves and on their foreheads. Later they made it on their forehead, breast, and shoulders while invoking God as Father, Son, and Holy Spirit.

The cross was first painted without figure or decoration. Later it was decorated with flowers to show that our life comes from the wood of the cross, and eventually Christ's body was represented on it.

The sign of the cross reminds us that our life comes through Jesus' death, and that he takes us into God's life as Trinity.

feel, God has been there and suffered that. For us, as for Jesus, these things are a path to life. Even death is not the end.

The crucifix hanging in the room does not say simply that Jesus once suffered as we do. It says that God suffers with us now, and we now share in Jesus' suffering. We do not just imagine Jesus in his pain, but can speak to the risen Jesus, who is now with us, still bearing his wounds. Our faith in Jesus is an invitation to conversation.

Of course, the crucifix is very realistic. The memory of Jesus also invites us to recognize the reality of our own lives. A Benedictine abbot once told his community that he did not agree with people who told him that at least things could not get any worse. He said that he always personally thought that things could get a great deal worse, and very often do. That is the reality of life, the rock on which we must stand if we are to find hope. The image of the Son of God suffering takes us on to that rock of reality, but it also assures us that we can trust God's promise that our lives and our world are destined for happiness. Nothing can separate us from the love of God.

46. HOW DOES JESUS HELP US COPE WITH OUR SINFULNESS?

ALL OF US EXPERIENCE, at times sharply and painfully, a gap in our lives between the person we think we are or would like to be and our actual behavior. We think we are reliable, and we betray a friend's confidence. We would like to be courageous, and when a friend needs us, we run away. We think of ourselves as good living people, and we find ourselves encouraging the most grotty and violent thoughts. If we believe in God, we find everything we touch is tainted and we are sinful.

We can respond by saying that we are really good, by believing the image we have of ourselves, denying all evidence to the contrary, and measuring ourselves by obedience to the rules we make for ourselves. Then, we blame those who fail by our standards. The problem is that deep down we do not believe the drum we beat for ourselves.

In this situation, Jesus makes a difference. We focus on God's personal love for us that never fails no matter what we do with our lives, and the incredible gift God has given us in our lives and in the world around us. We see God's great compassion for us in sharing our sinful lives and world in Jesus and suffering all the betrayal, coldness, and denial that we know in our own lives, and their murderous consequences. More than that, we see Jesus calling us to follow him, shonkiness and all.

When we are captured by God's compassion for us, we can look steadily at our own weaknesses—the things we do that shame us and from which we cringe—be sorry for them because they are so out of place in the beauty that God sees in our lives and world, and hope to live better. But we know that God's love for us does not depend on our living better—God loves us as we are.

That is why Pope Francis, when asked how he would describe himself, said he was a sinner to whom God is compassionate and whom he calls. For him, sin is not a reason for beating himself up; it is a reason for gratitude to the compassionate God who loves you despite your sinfulness. That makes a real difference.

FORGIVENESS

Reconciliation invites us to recognize ourselves as needy and broken. We can do that cheerfully because we know that we are forgiven and loved by God. God has plans for us, weak though we are, and invites us to be part of them.

Thus faith leads us to ask and receive forgiveness from others, and to thank God for forgiving us. We do this through words and gestures, not simply interiorly. Saying sorry, smiling forgiveness, and embracing after a quarrel are signs of reconciliation.

For Catholics, forgiveness and acknowledgment of brokenness are also expressed through rituals of penance, including particularly the sacrament of reconciliation.

After the Vietnam War, Nguyen Thi Lan left Vietnam by boat with her sister and two daughters to join her husband in Malaysia. The boat ran out of fuel, her food and water ran out, and the boat leader would not share what he had brought. She pleaded with him to give her children water, but he refused. Eventually, her children died in her arms. Later, her sister also died.

After the boat made land, they were taken to a camp. She was mad with grief and thought only of killing the boat leader. Then one day, she grew calm, and said to a friend, "I shall forgive this man." She added, "I want everyone to know that I forgive him." So she brought the man to the Sunday prayers and told him, "I forgive you." That day forgiveness freed her, her enemy, and those who heard her.

47. DOES IT MATTER THAT JESUS WILL COME AGAIN?

IN OUR SOCIETY TODAY, many people believe that we end with our death. If we believe that we will enjoy life after we die, we may be criticized for being escapists. People say our hope in the next life distracts us from our responsibility to make the world a better place. We can lose ourselves in the thought of eternity.

Our belief that we will rise with Jesus and inherit a transformed world when he comes again is not about escaping harsh reality. It simply provides a broader perspective from which we can see our lives and our world. Failure in our personal lives and in our plans is not the end of everything. There is a larger picture.

Our hope that Jesus will come again is not simply for our individual future. It is the hope that nothing good in our world, our lives, and our relationships will ever be lost. Our hope is for a transformed world. We cannot imagine it, but in it all that is good in our bodily world will be found

THE DAY OF JUDGMENT

Movies often depict the end of the world. They often borrow from the Bible, including *Final: The Rapture*, in which the faithful are taken into heaven and see the images from the Book of Revelation. Their popularity reflects our fears about the future.

The New Testament offers many vivid images of judgment. They invite us not to be preoccupied with the future, but to see the importance of the decisions we make. They invite us to live courageously, confident that God is with us.

These dramatic images of conflict also show us that not all the values of our society are those of Christ. To follow him is to be more than a patriotic citizen. Our faithfulness inevitably brings us into conflict with the values of our society.

and changed. It is a world in which God's love and desire for our happiness will triumph.

The center of this belief is Jesus. In the liturgy, we say that Christ will come again. When he rose bodily from the dead, his life was a promise of what will happen to us and to our world at the end of time. The stories of his rising point to the qualities that our life will have. It will be about victory over evil, companionship, joy and confidence, unlimited life, and the fulfillment of promises. We will be with Jesus and share in his transformed life.

The hope that Jesus will come again means that we don't have to be deadly serious. There is room for humor. We can certainly be serious about trying to live as Jesus did and about helping to change our world for the better. Yet our hope in Jesus' coming also allows us to acknowledge that our world and church are messy, and to laugh at our mistakes because they are not the last word. When Christ comes, the institutions of this world, with all their earnestness, will pass away, but all that is good in humanity and the world will remain in Christ.

48. WHY DO THE POOR MATTER TO JESUS?

PEOPLE OFTEN IDENTIFY Jesus with a concern for the poor. That is right. The words that sum up Jesus' message in Luke's Gospel are that *he has come to free captives and to bring Good News to the poor*. Throughout his mission, he is constantly described as noticing people who for others don't count, as going out to those from whom everybody else kept away, and as insisting that God loved dearly people whom others believed to be scorned by God. It was often the outsiders who believed in him and came close to him.

For Jesus, the poor were special because they could hear his message that God loved them and that his kingdom was close at hand. People who were comfortable did not hear this message because they could rely on themselves and assume that nothing would go wrong with their lives. They had a sense of entitlement. The poor were broken and knew their need, and

DOROTHY DAY

As a young journalist, Dorothy Day was appalled by the injustice she witnessed in New York City during the 1920s. She became a social activist, was often arrested, and later became a Catholic.

In 1933, she started a newspaper, *The Catholic Worker*, which promoted a just society. Challenged to put her ideas into practice, she also founded a house of hospitality. This radical way of following Jesus spread.

Dorothy Day remained a radical Catholic. Her pacifism in times of war cost her many followers, but she continued to reflect on the gospel and to struggle for people who were unjustly treated. She was frequently arrested.

She wrestled through her life with discerning what belonged to God and what belonged to Caesar and remains an inspiration for Catholics today.

were able to trust in Jesus' word that God's kingdom was near. They had no option but to hope in God.

For those of us who are not poor and broken and who can rely on our energy and resources to live securely, it is hard to trust in God deeply. We always like to keep our options open. Because we have options, we find it hard to believe deeply that God loves us, not for our obedience and our strengths, but in all our weakness and poverty. It is easy then for us to see the Church as a place for the comfortable and respectable, not for people who are broken and vulnerable.

That is why Pope Francis and others have insisted that the Church is the church of the poor and must go out of its comfort zone. When we do enter the world of those who are broken and needy and must trust in God to survive daily, we can recognize our own poverty and need for God, and we can find Jesus and his life real to us in those whom we meet. Our own compassion and care for the poor grows. Our own faith is awakened, and we do not judge others.

We also see that when Jesus spoke of the kingdom of God, it was above all a table at which the poor could find a seat. The business of his followers is to include the poor and the excluded.

49. TO WHOM DOES JESUS MAKE A DIFFERENCE?

IN A BOOK LIKE THIS one, Jesus can seem complicated. We have to think of Jesus in this and that way, pray in another way, and remember lots of things about him. But in reality, it is simple because it comes down to the relationship between people and Jesus, and the way in which Jesus captivates people's imagination and lives. So today I would like to look at one person to whom Jesus made a difference in surprising ways.

Khieu Sovan had nine children whom she kept alive during the Pol Pot years in Cambodia. No mean feat, when people were murdered arbitrarily or herded into camps, starved, made to work, and subjected to harsh punishment.

When I first met Sovan in a refugee camp, she was caring for many orphaned children as well as for her own children and was training young women in the camp to visit and help the poor families there. Her energy and generosity were astonishing.

THE COMMUNION OF SAINTS

The Nicene Creed professes the Communion of Saints. This rich phrase says we are not alone but are bound in faith to all Christians who have ever lived, not simply to the canonized saints, but to the hidden saints: our grandparents and friends in whom we saw Jesus' face.

We are also bound to our fellow believers today: to our Chaldean brothers and sisters so persecuted for their faith, and to the homeless poor in the barrios. And we are joined to our descendants whom God entrusts to us to pass on safely our world and our faith.

The Communion of Saints invites us to enlarge our imagination—to pray in thanks and compassion for all our brothers and sisters of all ages.

One day, Sovan told me that she was a great sinner. I told her I did not believe her. So she told me of her sin: she had stolen rice from the Khmer Rouge barns. This was a brave thing to do, for if she had been found out, she would have been beaten to death and her children would also have died. So I told her that, to keep her family from starving, it was not sinful to steal from the rice the officials were hoarding for themselves. She replied that she did not steal to feed her own children, but to support the elderly in the camp who were starving. Words failed me.

Sovan was a Buddhist at the time. She later became a Catholic and remains very active in the Church. For her, Jesus made a difference. It was not that she left a bad religion for a good one, a selfish way of life for an unselfish one, or falsehood for truth. In terms of goodness, truth, and faithfulness, she was a gift to us Catholics, not we to her.

For her, Jesus was a gift. He showed that the crazy love by which she lived was a reflection of God's love for us. He showed that when she responded with a self-forgetting love to the misery and brutality of life in Cambodia, she was unknowingly following his way. In the lives of those who followed Jesus, she saw the hope that evil and brutality she had known were conquered by Jesus' rising from the dead.

50. WHY IS JESUS GOOD NEWS?

FOR THE EARLY CHRISTIANS, Jesus was simply gospel: good news. Usually good news seems particularly good when we have been waiting. If we are waiting and hoping for someone to love, the arrival of that someone seems to be great news. If we are hanging out for the end of a war, the news of peace that promises security and a life for our children is tremendous news.

Good news seems particularly good when we are on a journey. If we are lost without a compass, the sight of the sea or of a familiar mountain is great news. Good news always comes as surprise.

That was what Jesus was like for the early Christians. They were waiting for God to come into their world. In Jesus, they knew that God had come. They were astonished that God came through his death and delighted that their own journey would end in rising with him in a transformed world.

JOY

Jesus is Good News. Any good news makes us happy. The joy of the gospel is not just natural bubbliness. It is the deep joy that God loves us and that Jesus' way is life-giving.

We catch glimpses of joy in the humor of extraordinary Christians. St. Thomas More, for example, asked his executioner not to cut off his beard as well as his head because it had not offended the king. Many others who can laugh in the midst of great suffering echo his spirit.

Pope Francis associates joy with spreading the good news. He urges us not to be sourpusses or to lay heavy burdens on other people. People learn fear, but they catch joy.

That is what Jesus is like for those who share the faith of the early Church. On our journey through life, we wait to find meaning, to find love we can give and receive, to find reasons for living, to find patience in suffering. When we are waiting, we can be surprised to find God's intimate love for us in Jesus.

Jesus is also good news for us when we are weary, drudging through our days, living in fear, and enslaved to duty and to other people's expectations of us. We can discover with surprise that God loves us, not because we fulfill expectations or obey laws, but because we are precious in God's sight, sinfulness and all. Jesus died for us as sinners. To discover Jesus as freedom sets us free from fear, free to live. That is great good news.

When we are lonely and longing for friends and the company of people who share our dreams, Jesus is also good news. He came to reconcile people who are divided, and connects us with people who share faith in God's love for us.

Jesus is also good news when we want to make a difference. Jesus draws our attention to the marginal and neglected people on the edge of our world and invites us to follow him in feeding, nursing, and nuturing them. To be invited to follow Jesus on his path is really good news. We will surely share his toil and pain, but we also know that we will share his victory.